Scavenge Your Way To Real Estate Riches

Capturing the Scavenger Mindset and Employing the Hands on Approach

Steve Ames

Scavenger House Publishing
11 South 8th Avenue
Marshalltown, Iowa 50158

ISBN: 0989599116
ISBN 13: 9780989599115

Table of Contents

Introduction

After having driven all the way from Iowa to Florida to meet the editor, Adam, of my first book, *Scavenge Your Way to Wealth*, the very first words he said to me, even before we had the chance to properly introduce ourselves, were, "Gosh, Steve, you sure have broadened the definition of the term *to scavenge*!"

It was almost as though he was convinced that *Webster's Dictionary* would rewrite the definition of "to scavenge" from that moment onward. Now that I've written this book, the second book on such a topic, and now that I've established myself as an expert and made "scavenging" my brand, as in the "Guru of Scavenging," I'll surely have to send Adam a copy of this book, just to hear his reaction!

Now, let's examine just how broad my concept of scavenging really is. I came from a large family of dump pickers, or scavengers; needless to say, this has given me the inspiration to establish myself as an authority in this field. Going back to 1954, when I was only four years old, our family found itself without any income. My dad went from having an above-average income working in a stone mill to abruptly finding himself totally unemployable due to the fact that his lungs had filled up with stone dust. We found ourselves just about as close to being destitute as you can get, not knowing at the time that years would pass before my dad would receive his first Social Security disability check.

At that moment we took to scavenging, routinely making our rounds to all the city and county dumps in the area, fishing out anything of value. We mainly found scrap pieces of metal of all sizes and descriptions that we took to the nearest salvage yard to be recycled, exchanging them for cash, which allowed us to barely survive, but only by the skin of our teeth. Thank God for hand-me-downs, trot lines, large gardens, goats, runt pigs that we nurtured to full size before butchering, and all the city and county dumps.

All those trips to the area dumps made me focus on value, which helped me greatly as I later would become heavily involved in the real estate business. I used this knowledge to help me determine the real value of properties, particularly the handyman, fixer-upper types of houses that could be bought cheap, which by and large were passed over by the majority of other investors. In this book, I will teach you all the scavenging techniques necessary to rehab fixer-upper properties, as well as rehab any and all other types of properties, which will allow you to build equity ever so quickly, at a far more rapid pace than following other conventional forms of rehabbing. Ultimately this will shave months and years off the time needed to reach your goals.

Before you get started on your quest to pluck out an uncountable number of "golden nuggets" from the following 12 chapters—which should help make or save you "boatloads" of money—let me put in my own words all the ways the word *scavenging* can be defined, applied, or interpreted in this book.

My definition of the term *scavenge* is as follows:

To create something out of nothing;

To economize, or make more economical any product or procedure;

To utilize, discover, re-purpose, reclaim, or take advantage of something (material, person, written or verbal, etc.) that has been overlooked, discarded, or abandoned so that its life may be extended and/or put to use in a new found way.

Like a magician pulling coins out of thin air, you are creating value. You are discovering and unlocking the *Hidden Value* in items or situations that will accelerate equity appreciation in all types of real estate endeavors. It doesn't always take money to make money. Sometimes it just takes a good idea or bit of creative thrift. The successful scavenger *needs* to do this at every opportunity. Necessity is not just the Mother of Invention—it is also the Mother of Profit, and besides, it can be a lot of *fun*. These behaviors result in the greatest possible value to the scavenger with the smallest possible dollar investment.

By the way, my scavenging techniques are not only about materials that are recycled or re-purposed, but also include obtaining and utilizing brand-new scavenged materials from store closings, total liquidation sales, factory overstocks and closeouts, and so forth. I will soon tell you about this in more detail.

When the principals of this book, *Scavenge Your Way to Real Estate Riches*, are applied consistently over time, they can bring about a totally new mind-set and mentality that allows real estate investors to quickly build equity, which can be leveraged to increase asset holdings. Furthermore, the "scavenging mind-set" provides a foundation for discovering value in other disciplines as well, such as health, finance, and shopping, just to name a few.

In short, instead of pulling hard-won dollars out of your bank account to invest and build wealth during your life, pull as many of them as you can out of thin air like I do. You will be richer for it—both in money and in pride of accomplishment.

I hope you enjoy the book.

One

Scavenging the Down Payment

Now that you have somehow declared real estate as a topic that interests you and you find yourself close to making your first investment, of course your next step is determining a method of down payment. Though on rare occasions you may find a property you're able to purchase without a down payment, that's something that can't be counted on regularly. Your plan to purchase investment property must include some method of down payment.

If you read my first book, *Scavenge Your Way to Wealth*, you will remember I scavenged the down payment for the purchase of my first property by doing contract painting. I kept working at my main job, or day job, as a teacher, which paid the bills. Then, while retaining my day job, I did contract painting in the evenings, on weekends, at holiday time, and during summer vacations. In just a few months, back in 1977, I saved $5,500 and bought my first property for $13,000. Precisely what I did then is the very thing I'm advocating you do now—work a second job while retaining your primary job, and not only that, but work by the contract, not by the hour.

The reasoning behind this is as follows:

People are made uncomfortable by the unknown.

By offering a Flat Fee—rather than an Hourly Rate and an open-ended financial risk caused by the unknown time factor—you are offering them firm certainty. The convenient result for the Scavenger is that people will happily accept a higher but certain Flat Rate over the lower but open-ended hourly situation. In other words, *they will actually be happier paying more!* How great is that? By doing this, the Scavenger will make *much* more money as a rookie in their new trade than otherwise.

For example, if you were to bid $325 to paint the trim, the fascia and basement foundation of a house, and completed the work in 6 hours, the customer would not hesitate to pay you the contracted price. However, a property owner would usually expect to pay a casual laborer no more than $12.50 an hour for the exact same task, which would result in a paycheck of only $75.

Though there are many methods of creating a down payment, other than cash, that we will get to later in the chapter, for now I'd like to inspire you to concentrate on various ways to put your hands on pure cash, to fulfill your down payment needs, by selecting at least one of the many options I'm about to reveal. Before I begin giving you examples of that, please let me reiterate, one more time, that you should *never* find yourself accepting part-time employment, where you have to trade your hours worked for dollars earned.

You must create a business you can do part-time and be your own boss. In other words, always work by contract, never by the hour! As I'm about to show you through examples, contracting will allow you to build reserves of cash quite quickly. Also, coming up with the down payment all by yourself—in other words, without including partners—will make you reign as king, and your profits will be all yours, never having to be shared with anyone. And obviously, without partners, your decisions will never be subjected to rejection. Only you will make them, and they always will be final.

I've broken down the various methods of building quick reserves of cash into two categories, between the more physical and the less physical types of jobs.

Paying Cash as a Method of Down Payment

All my life I've been about a 50-50 split between the brute strength grunt who takes the bull by the horns and the intellectual type of person who tries to find the less physical way to get something done.

I find that doing the physical work yourself can help you to better understand more efficient ways of doing things when it's necessary to delegate, or contract out the labor. As such, sometimes a mixture of managerial and direct working experience is not a bad thing.

Therefore, let's now have a look at some of these more physical types of jobs you could scavenge for yourself, by creating them very economically, with very little spent for start-up costs, to build cash reserves "lightning fast," as I like to say, while at the same time retaining your primary employment. Though I could write an entire book on this topic, I will try to chose only examples of quick-starting businesses that will give you enough suitable options to allow you to immediately start a new "cash machine" business without delay.

Asphalt Seal Coating

Asphalt seal coating is only one of many examples I'm about to give you of the more physical types of contract labor businesses that have great earning potential. Your start-up costs would be for the purchase of a few five-gallon buckets of sealant, a paint roller, a roller cover and handle, a squeegee and, if you really wanted to stretch it, you could buy a few wooden stakes and a medium-sized roll of caution tape, all for the miniscule amount of less than $50.

Even if you have not had much business experience, knocking on a few doors and doing a driveway or two for free, less the cost of materials, would not set you back much. Then, by that time, you would be supercharged and ready to go make some serious money. Since the topic is doing contract work for cash, you must be asking yourself, "Just how much could a person make?" Let's say you chose a three-month period in which you averaged eight driveways per week, one or so per evening and a few on Saturdays, at $200 profit per driveway, while still maintaining your primary employment.

Eight jobs per week times $200 is $1,600, times 13 weeks (about a quarter of a year), equals $20,800. Now, let me ask you this. Would $20,800 be enough cash to make the down payment on an average rental house, even if you had to finance the purchase through a bank and pay 20% down?

Absolutely it would be!

Before we get to the less physical types of jobs that will also allow you to put down-payment cash together in a very short period of time, let me give you several more prime examples of other more physical jobs. Remember, too, it's always best, while doing any kind of contract labor, to have the simple terms and conditions written down in the form of a contract that's signed and dated by both you and the customer. This would include you being able to show some form of liability insurance to cover any potential damages to the property, or injuries to anyone at the worksite.

Lawn Care Service

Lawn mowing could be expanded to include fertilizing, weed killing, hedge trimming, and so forth. I mowed 22 lawns each week at the age of 15 in the mid-1960s with only my push mower and averaged $100 per week, when wages were at least 10 times less than today. By including with the mowing some weed killer and fertilizer, you could add greatly to your profit, something I never even thought about way back then.

Contract Painting

This type of work was something I did on a part-time basis for many years, and it helped me work my way through college. The key here is to contract the work, as I advocate throughout. In other words, never work by the hour. Though more can be made spraying, there's plenty that can also be made by rolling and brushing if you don't want to take the time to learn how to spray.

Gutter Cleaning Services

There are always homeowners looking for someone to perform the service of cleaning downspouts and gutters. Like painting and most types of cleaning, your start-up costs are very minimal.

Pressure Washing Services

Homeowners and commercial businesses alike will employ you to clean the exterior of their houses and businesses by means of power/pressure washing. There's always a need for this service, whether you're pressure washing only decks, patios, and foundations or doing whole vinyl, brick, stone, stucco, or wood exteriors, whether it be of homes or businesses.

Window Cleaning Services

Whether it's an interior window cleaning service or an exterior window cleaning service, there's always a demand. I've known a few contractors involved in this type of business over the years, and they've done quite well! Don't worry about how much to charge. You'll be able to figure that out as you go along. However, always try to average the equivalent of $100 per hour at a minimum. Eventually, you'll figure out exactly how much to charge per window.

Other more physical types of jobs you can contract on a part-time basis are as follows:

- Metals scavenging/salvaging
- Hauling
- Handyman services
- Auto grooming house to house
- Landscape services
- House cleaning services
- Insulating services
- Carpet cleaning
- Carpet dyeing

Now let's look at some of the less physical types of jobs that also will allow you to put together a cash down payment in a relatively short period of time while maintaining your primary source of income.

Computer House Doctor

If you're good with computers, why not start a house-to-house computer defragging/antivirus service? We just had it done to our house desktop computer for $100, and the guy was long gone before one hour had passed. This seems to be the type of business whereby you average a few service calls each evening plus a few more on Saturdays, and a screwdriver would be your only start-up cost.

Tutoring

Have you ever thought about conducting special classes or giving any type of lessons? Are you any good at playing the piano or guitar, understanding computers, or speaking a foreign language? If the answer to any of those questions is yes, then you have a steady flow of extra cash just waiting for the taking, as my dad used to say. Because I'm fluent in Spanish and have given lessons as well as weekend seminars, I know that the opportunities are robust!

Teaching a group of 5-15 students, for example, and at times coaching each student on a one to one basis as needed within the same group of students, allows you to be paid for contracted services at a much higher rate of pay.

Website Builder

If you're good with computers, chances are you can already build, or learn to build, websites. I've been told that in the Midwest, where I live, you can easily earn $100 to $200 per hour at it.

Tour Guide

Many communities, or those within shouting distance of where you are, are in need of a tour guide. Buy a good cellular phone if you don't already have one, read up on the area at the public library, announce your services to the community, and, poof, you're in business. Though I didn't actually do this type of work, I was asked to many times by guests who frequented the five-star hotel where I swam daily while living and working in South America as a young man. I'm still kicking myself for not capitalizing on such a grand opportunity!

Affiliate Marketer

Have you ever considered being an affiliate marketer? People sell other people's stuff everyday on the Internet and make tons of money at it. You don't even need a list of subscribers, a product, or a website. Just find an online product you know well, and use. You can comment on why you like this product, or possibly mention it in your online articles, blogs, tweets, etc., and have links to these products. You are then paid according to the number of customers who click on the links, and/or who buy products.

Security Systems Installer

If you are the slightest bit technological, you could very easily install three to four cameras, install the monitor, and do the wiring, completing this type of installation. Many homeowners, small business owners, and even apartment dwellers in this day and age have a desire for more security. Nowadays, many of these systems can even be monitored on one's cell phone and are easy to install. So, go provide a service to those feeding-frenzy customers and make some money!

Other less physical types of jobs you can contract on a part-time basis include these:

- Bookkeeping Services
- Social media consultant
- Filming and photography services
- Online programming services
- e-book salesperson
- Home entertainment systems installer

Other Common Methods That Suffice for the Down Payment

Let's have a look at various other methods to scavenge the down payment. The cash approach to satisfy the down payment is quick and easy, if you have the cash. But what if another good deal comes along and you've not had time to accumulate additional cash to consolidate the next deal? Instead of utilizing the more conventional cash approach that we just covered, I would encourage you to "think outside the box" and look for other ways to come up with the down payment.

The Sweat Equity Approach

In this method, if you're flat broke but have good manual skills and can ask a half dozen people or so to write up testimonials proclaiming your impeccable workmanship, honesty, and integrity, then you very possibly could become a partial owner in a great property, such as an apartment complex. Many high-income people such as doctors, lawyers, dentists, business owners, and so forth would jump at the chance to partner up with you. For example, if you'd simply be willing to manage and do all the maintenance on a 20 to 40 unit apartment building for three to five years, in exchange for free rent and a minimal wage during that period of time, they just might sign an agreement to give you 25% or more of the equity buildup when the property is sold. You could be convincing enough by showing them what the average management company would charge for the same size complex. You could have it all penciled out to bolster your case and be convincing of your self-worth.

Another way to look at it is this: Where else might you be able to realize a net gain of $75,000 to $150,000 or more during that same period of time? And, if you're very selective, that kind of money should be enough for you to pay most of the down payment on a 50-unit apartment complex or the whole down payment on a 25-unit complex. If you are a hard-working, very hands-on type of person, as I was, but have none of your own money for property acquisition, then this plan of action might be a great option you should consider. You'd only have to convince a would-be partner that you could manage the complex, hold the line on material expenses, and slash labor costs, adding greatly to the profitability and ongoing appreciation.

Family, Friends, and Acquaintances

Roughly 20 years ago, I ran across the cutest little one-bedroom house I'd ever seen for only $4,000. At that very moment, I'd just paid property taxes and income taxes and had a ton of other expenses. I struggled to put my hands on $4,000, even though I was just baby steps away from my net worth being $1,000,000! Can you imagine that? But, yes, it was true. Anyway, about that same time, one of my two mentors offered to loan me the money. He knew I could pay him back in a few weeks and loaned me the money, just on a handshake.

Also, don't forget that friends and family might decide to cosign a loan with you, especially if you offer to put their names on the title, until the loan is paid back in full. Be completely honest with them, explain just how profitable the deal will be, go through an attorney, and even have an attorney's sample contract drawn up ahead of time to show them. Chances are you'll find all the down-payment money you need, and then some.

Seller Financing

Seller financing is exactly what the term indicates. In order to complete a sale to the buyer, the seller finances all or part of the transaction. In other words the seller may finance only the down pay-ment and let a bank finance the rest, or the seller may finance 100% of the deal. In the case of 100% financing, the seller may decide to give the buyer two to five years to make monthly payments on the property before calling the note due. Calling the note due after only a few short years is commonly known as a balloon payment, though during that time frame the buyer is expected to repair his or her credit before financing the same property again, this time through a bank or another type of lending institution.

In the case of the seller providing only the down-payment por-tion of the loan to the buyer, the seller is given a second mortgage by the buyer, in which he or she receives monthly payments (though sometimes quarterly or biannual payments) until the down-payment portion is paid back in full or until the payment balloons, depending upon the way the second mortgage is written.

I personally have used seller financing on a few occasions, including one purchase I made of a four-unit apartment building back in the 1980s. The owner, who was on her way to a nursing home, agreed to finance the entire purchase for me, with the exception of a $2,000 down payment. As luck would have it, her attorney even gave me considerable time to put the down payment together, even though I had long before taken possession of the property. Just a few years after the purchase, the lady passed away. Then, within days of her passing, because her children were anxious to settle the estate, her attorney offered to cut the remainder of the loan in half as long as I could pay off the balance. Sure enough, my friendly banker complied with my request, pulling the necessary equity out of that same property, to pay off the four-plex, and the rest is history. What a golden nugget and cash cow that property has been for me all these years! These types of experiences will also come your way. Just hang in there and keep your head in the game.

In case you're wondering, the $3,500,000 purchase I made in 2008 of a 108-unit complex, where the seller financed for me $350,000, or 10%, has been my biggest seller-financed transaction to date. I gave the seller a second mortgage and agreed to make payments to him monthly, for five years, interest only, at a 6% interest rate. I was to pay him back in full after five years but refinanced the property and paid him off after only three and a half years. Upon refinancing the property, the 10% I'd borrowed from the seller ($350,000) was incorporated or absorbed in the newly rewritten loan, eliminating the second mortgage.

Realtors

There are many realtors out there who are willing to use their sales commission to help finance a deal and perhaps even chip in additional money.

At that point they will either become a partner or receive monthly payments from you until the money they invested is paid back. Also, if you have carefully chosen a realtor who is willing to work with you in such a creative financing maneuver, chances are that person will go out of his or her way to cherry-pick the best deal on the market at the time, in the area you wish to buy, and likewise will use his or her experience to get the best terms possible.

Though I personally never called upon a realtor to help finance or be a partner in any of my deals, I did have a realtor come to me and offer to do both. I was looking to buy a multi-hundred-unit complex in Texas a few years ago. The realtor helping me find a property in foreclosure or bankruptcy said to me right out of the blue, "Steve, would you consider letting me be your 50-50 partner in this deal?" Though he was highly successful in commercial real estate sales, the bank that was to finance the deal deemed him too big a credit risk because of previously lingering income tax issues and disallowed him from being my partner. However, he was only a short time away from getting his credit cleaned up and was very willing to put up half the down payment and be my partner, especially since I had so much experience in the rental business.

Home Equity Loans

Whether you're just starting out in real estate investing or have been doing it a long while, pulling cash out of the equity in your home is a very viable alternative. If you have any equity at all in your home, you should be able to access it rather quickly, 75% to 80% LTV—loan to value, that is—for buying or rehabbing an investment property or doing both. I, myself, have asked for and received a home equity loan to help with investing on three or four occasions. In case you're unsure as to how it works, I'll give you the following example. Let's say your house is worth $100,000 but you still owe $60,000 on it. Therefore, your real equity only amounts to $40,000.

However, since most banks will allow you to borrow no more than 75% LTV, you will be able to borrow no more than $30,000 of your equity of $40,000, less the cost of the appraisal and other closing costs.

Trade

Another way to scavenge the purchase of a property, or take possession without having to come up with any cash on the buyer's behalf, is to trade the seller something that will suffice for the down payment. For example, let's say you have found a house valued at $40,000 but have no down-payment money. However, in lieu of cash, the seller agrees to accept a form of trade, equivalent in value to roughly $4,000, which would be the same as receiving a 10% down payment, once the traded item or items are professionally evaluated. The following are examples of things the buyer might offer to the seller to satisfy the down payment and take possession of the property:

- Antiques of any kind or items known to be collectibles
- A vacant lot, a mobile home, a river cabin, a lake house, etc.
- Certain rare coins or collections of rare items
- Jewelry
- Gold, silver, or other precious metals
- A boat, car, truck, motorcycle, etc.
- A motor home
- A camper
- Rare paintings, musical instruments, fire arms, furniture, etc.

Repair Allowance

This is a way to scavenge money at closing for the down payment and sometimes have enough additional money for repairs, money that you never would have seen otherwise. Simply walk the property you plan to buy, listing all the things within reason that need to be repaired. This, by the way, is known as *doing the due diligence*. When the due diligence is complete, present the list to the owner. Tell him you'll give him the full agreed-upon negotiated price for the property but that, on the day of closing, he'll have to give you a check for the repairs, known as a repair allowance.

If the seller says no, simply try to renegotiate the price, then add the cost for the repairs on to the end of the agreed-upon price. Most banks will loan you money based on the ARV (after repaired value) of the property, of course anticipating the increased value of the property after the repairs are done.

In any event, if the seller is even the slightest bit motivated to sell, the two of you should be able to come up with an agreed-upon price that satisfies the two of you, as well as the bank.

To put even more money in your pocket, if the property is two to four units, you usually can cut down the down payment to the bank by declaring that the property will be owner occupied. In other words, you declare that you intend to live there. Some banks might "let you lie to them" about "being owner occupied." Just be prepared to move into the place, at least for a while.

Sell Part of the Seller's Property

Oftentimes the property you're interested in buying consists of an oversized lot or comes with an additional partial or two of land. In this case, you might be able to arrange the sale of that extra lot or two to an adjacent landlord, or to anyone, and have the sale transact on the day of the closing. Therefore, you would easily have your scavenged down payment at hand, buying the property at no out-of-pocket expense to you.

To enhance the interest of the neighbor, adjacent landlord, or would-be buyer, predetermine the value of the lot or lots, then offer to sell at a considerably reduced rate—that is, if you can't conclude the sale at "full price."

Also, for those of you involved in buying multifamily complexes, many times you can employ this same idea. For example, since apartment complexes can be legally and easily converted to individually owned condos, you could arrange for the sale of these units simply by stretching out your possession date to 90 or 120 days, giving you ample opportunity to find buyers. These buyers could then sign separate contracts or offers to buy, which you will have drawn up by an attorney, legitimizing you receiving-down-payment money to accepting payment in full, on or before your closing day.

Does this sound unusual? Believe it or not, it's done all the time. Just begin to fill your thoughts with these types of scavengable ideas. They will put an indelible smile on your face, continually, until you're in heaven!

Assumption of Mortgage

I once assumed a mortgage on an eight-unit complex that was owned by the president of our local Savings and Loan, whose favorite hobby was rehabbing older properties, the same as mine. Luckily for me, he was so anxious to retire and just get the sale behind him that I gave him no down payment. In other words, he just gave me the equity he had built up in the property, not forcing me to buy out his equity or offer him a second mortgage as compensation. After one year, another bank across town recognized my equity in the property and decided it was just enough to be able to give me a new mortgage, without me having to come up with a down payment. How about that for being able to scavenge a $100,000 property! Here's another little golden nugget for you. Always recognize that having good chemistry with those with whom you become aligned never hurts and usually pays huge dividends at a minimum!

Wraparound Mortgage

This is a quick way to lay claim to a property while having little to no down payment. This transaction usually appeals more to those who are turned down by most conventional lenders because of poor or damaged credit but can at times work in favor of the investor acquiring properties, of course, if the terms are somewhat favorable. For example, during a time of inflation, if you could get control of a property, let's say from $0 to $4,000 down, even if the rate you are charged for interest is three points higher than the bank's rate, it still could be a profitable transaction, allowing tenants to pay down the mortgage.

In my opinion, a wrap is a good scavengable way to take owner- ship of a property if you as a buyer don't have to pay for too much blue sky—in other words, if the actual value isn't exaggerated—and if the amount of interest you pay on the spread is not unreasonable.

Credit Card Checks

Using credit card checks is a quick and easy way to stick a 5% to 10% down payment onto a cheap to moderately priced house, like those many little bulldoze-able shacks I bought over the years that made me so much money.

That 0% interest for 12 to 18 months with only a 3% transac- tion fee can be very attractive, but be careful! If you don't constantly make yourself aware of when the rate dramatically increases, you could find yourself paying tons of interest, which tends to gobble up profits pretty fast.

I would beg of you to use credit card checks only if you have a strategy to pay them off in the not-so-distant future and are com- pletely able to wipe the slate clean. Just be careful to not let the interest rate devour you like a cancer without a cure.

Land Contracts

Buying on contract, as it's called, is another easy and uncomplicated way to scavenge the purchase of a property, oftentimes needing little or no money as a down payment. In this type of contract, also known as a contract for deed or agreement for deed, the seller creates a loan and finances the transaction for the buyer. This non-conventional type of sales agreement can be hugely advantageous to buyers who can't qualify for normal financing through a formal lending institution, perhaps because of very unfortunate circumstances that may have damaged their credit. There are many other reasons why using this buying method is seen as popular and favorable, regardless of how good or bad your credit. The following is a list of some of those reasons:

- Obtaining possession is quicker than through conventional methods
- Getting the seller to accept your terms is far more likely
- Little or no down payment might be acceptable
- Unestablished or poor or damaged credit may not be an issue
- Granting possession can be instant or, as I like to say, "lightning fast"
- May realize closing cost savings and fewer complications
- Can be written or modified by any seller or buyer
- Any variety of repayment plans are available, such as:

  1. Possibly paying interest only six months to three years before P&I kick in
  2. Amortization schedules can be written up any which way
  3. A short-term or long-term balloon payment, or none at all, could be called for
  4. The buyer and seller may decide to not record the contract, citing advantages for both parties
  5. The contract may allow the buyer to assign his or her interest in the property to yet another buyer before the loan is paid in full

Since all contracts have some legal ambiguities, my advice is to always go through a real estate attorney to greatly reduce, if not eliminate, the possibility of any future disagreement or lawsuit because of the way your particular contract was put together.

I personally have used land contracts many times to buy and sell properties, including a $10,000 shack I bought just last year, putting only $1,000 down upon taking possession. Though there has been some talk of eliminating the land contract, probably because many if not most are drawn up without the help of an attorney, leading to uncountable ramifications, it doesn't look probable.

However, in my opinion, as long as we human beings have the desire to continue to create simple signed and dated agreements, recognized by the courts throughout the land as true and binding, eliminating simple land contracts will be impossible.

Though there are countless ways to scavenge the purchase of a property, I've tried to comment in detail on some personal experiences and on some of the more common ways to do so. The following list displays even more commonly known ways to unconventionally acquire, or "scavenge the purchase of," property:

- Private lenders (other than family and friends)
- Hard money lenders
- Signature loans
- Private mortgages
- Short sales
- Transactional funding
- Asset stripping
- Land trusts
- Equity share with investor(s)
- Subject to
- Equity share with owner(s)
- Simultaneous closings
- Lease options
- Rehab contractors
- First-time home-buyer programs
- 401k borrowing
- Local government down-payment assistance programs

- Other investors
- Future profit acquisitions
- Sale of existing resources (on the property)
- Line of credit
- Government grants

Key Points

- Cash is only one of many methods whereby a down payment can be created.
- Never trade hours for dollars; work by contract!
- Be your own boss at a part-time business while you retain your regular job.
- Avoid asking partners for down-payment cash as you get started, which gives you full control of profits and decisions, allowing you to be more drawn to your investments.
- Realize that creating down-payment money is between "more physical" and "less physical" types of jobs.
- Having a written contract for each job and being able to show some form of liability insurance is always best.
- Asphalt seal coating is a high-paying part-time business you could easily create for less than $50, with a potential for saving $20,800 in three months.
- Simple lawn mowing, including fertilizing and weed killing, is another part-time business worth considering.
- Much money can be made through contract painting, including by rolling and brushing, and even more by spraying.
- Gutter cleaning is always in demand, and start-up costs are minimal.
- Homeowners and commercial businesses will always hire you to do some form of power/pressure washing.
- Window cleaning services are always in demand, and, though you charge by the number of windows cleaned, you average a minimum of $100 per hour.
- Other very high-paying "physical" part-time jobs are metals scavenging/salvaging, hauling, handyman services, auto

grooming, house-to-house landscape services, house cleaning services, insulating services, carpet cleaning, carpet dyeing, etc.

- Being a computer house doctor is one of many "less physical" businesses; it consists of defragging and antivirus services and is well paying, with minimal start-up costs.
- Tutoring will bring in a flow of extra cash if you're good at a foreign language, computers, or instrumental music.
- If you're good at building websites, $100 to $200 per hour might just be awaiting you.
- Many communities need tour guides, and for the cost of a cellular phone, you can be in business.
- Tons of money can be made as an affiliate marketer, which involves selling other people's stuff on the Internet without subscribers, a product, or a website.
- You can make some good money by being a security systems installer if you can do simple wiring, plus installing cameras and a monitor.
- Other "less physical" types of jobs available to you are bookkeeping services, social media consultant, filming and photography services, online programming services, e-book salesperson, home entertainment systems installer, etc.
- There are many other common methods to satisfy the down payment other than using cash.
- If you have great maintenance and management skills, you could become part owner of an apartment complex, exchanging your skills, in a sense, for the down payment and possibly gaining quicker equity than other means.
- Family, friends, and acquaintances might loan you the money, especially if you offer to put their name(s) on the title until it's paid back.
- Seller financing is still another way to account for the down payment. Upon getting the asking price, the seller may loan you enough cash at closing to cover the down payment, creating a second mortgage whereby you'd make additional monthly payments until the second mortgage is paid off.

- Golden nugget and cash cow properties will eventually come your way if you just hang in there and keep your head in the game.
- You will find realtors who will offer their sales commissions and additional money to help you finance a deal, oftentimes finding (the both of you) the best deal out there.
- You can borrow money from yourself by utilizing a home equity loan, usually borrowing as much as 75% to 80% of the equity in your home.
- Many sellers will accept an object for the down payment, such as jewelry, antiques, etc., equivalent to 10% to 20%.
- At closing, many owners will give you a repair allowance, consisting of a dollar amount equal to the needed repairs on the property, that can be used for the down payment.
- At closing you can have prearranged to sell off an adjacent lot of the property you're buying to suffice for the down payment or sell, at closing, apartments converted to condos or vice-versa.
- A mortgage sometimes does not require a down payment, especially if you find the right deal and you discover you have good chemistry with the seller.
- Even wraparound mortgages can be acquired with little to no down payment, at times making the purchase worthwhile for the investor.
- Credit card checks can be a beneficial way to create a down payment, all the while staying conscious of the dramatic interest rate rise coming down the road, of course.
- Using a land contract to purchase property may entail coming up with little to no down payment and a whole host of other positives, such as those listed in this chapter.
- Other ways to scavenge the down payment and/or the purchase of properties are listed at the end of this chapter. A few of those examples are as follows: by way of private lenders, signature loans, asset stripping, simultaneous closings, 401k borrowing, lines of credit, etc.

Two

Scavenging
the Purchase

Countless "gurus" in the real estate education and seminar market sell sure-fire get-rich-quick "no money down" buying schemes. What they don't tell their students is that while, yes, some of these are perfectly legitimate techniques, they don't pop up all that often. Think about it, if everybody in the market is ready to pounce on such deals, how many can there really be to go around? So yes, as a scavenger, you too, will jump on such deals when they come up, but you can't rely on them as a steady-eddy way to acquire property on the scale you will desire.

Fortunately for you, my student scavenger, I have something even better than the far too rare occurrence of a desperate seller, begging you to please take the years of accumulated equity (in their for-sale-property), off their hands for zero money down. In this chapter I introduce to you one of the cornerstone techniques I use to scavenge down payments for properties. I have used it countless times. If you pull this one out of your own personal scavenging magic bag, you truly will be pulling down-payments out of thin air like I do, and will always be able to make almost any of your deals "no-money-down."

Cross-Collateralization

The name might sound complicated, but it is not. It is simply the process of using accumulated equity in one or more properties you already own as collateral for the down-payment for a new property you want to get. Banks are perfectly happy to do this type of transaction. Providing you have enough equity, then no cash is involved—just your signature. Poof, magic.

Just imagine: you made a great scavenge on your last property and already have a healthy amount of equity in it, because you employed the techniques I have taught you to the hilt. Now, the magic you just worked is carried forward and amplified. The more equity you can create now, the more equity you'll have available in later deals, through the magic of cross-collateralization.

Though you must find a way to come up with the down payment to buy your first property, from that moment on you'll always have collateral to buy future properties. From that point forward, finding the down payment will no longer be necessary. In other words, if you had to sell it the next day, you should be able to at least get back out of the property the value of your down payment, which is your property's collateral.

So, assuming you retain that first property for a year, during which time you modernize it through renovations, you see the mortgage pay down some, and you watch it appreciate in value through improvements, coupled with some inflation, you not only have in the property the simple collateral created by your down payment, but you have growing, ongoing collateral. This self-perpetuating, continually growing, and ongoing collateral, provided me the leverage I needed to continue to buy properties with just my signature, and allowed me to explode my investment property portfolio ever so rapidly.

Scavenging the purchase through cross-collateralization—perhaps a pretty big word for a new investor, but one you should be aware of—allowed me to buy property after property using none of my own money. It also allowed me to pull additional funds out of the transaction to rehab the property at hand, whereby, in most cases, I never had to "use my own money" even for rehabbing. In other words, I rarely had to disturb the funds I personally had set aside in different savings and checking accounts for other things.

Now, you must be asking yourself, "How successful can I be and how fast can I go at building my investment portfolio using this method of transferring collateral?" My answer to that is to make purchases as often as you can, like in anything else, as long as you can keep the stress level at a manageable pace.

At this time let me show you a potential good pattern for a beginning investor to follow, following my "scavenge the purchase" method. Let's say you decide upon one of the down-payment methods I laid out in chapter 1 and bought your first property. If you're new to rehabbing give yourself one whole year to, little by little, modernize the house, while it is being lived in by your first round of tenants. This might sound a little tricky, but it's necessary to get tenants to occupy the dwelling as soon after taking possession as possible. You'll need the rental income to make your monthly payments and do renovations with whatever amount is left over. Rehabbing while the house is occupied is rarely an issue because tenants always enjoy seeing the improvements.

After about one year from purchasing your first rental house, your rehab should be complete. At this time go to the bank where you do the most business, find a loan officer, and explain your situation. Your dialogue with him should go something like this:

> Hi, Bill, I'm John Doe. I've been a customer here
> at this bank since 2012 and have begun to invest in
> income property. I was hoping to talk to you about
> having my rental property appraised. I have another
> property in mind to buy and would like to utilize the

equity in my current rental property to be able to buy a second property. Do you have time to visit with me now, or do you need me to come back at a different time?

If you maintain at least an average credit score and don't have a history of delinquent payments, banks overwhelmingly will try to meet your needs. Why? Because banks always need good customers. Obviously, that's how they make their money or they wouldn't be in business!

OK, now one year has passed, and you're about to take possession of your second income property. At this time you'll start to ask yourself questions like, "Will I be able to continually make purchases of these types of properties every four to six months, or should I stay in the rhythm of buying only one each year?" Going back to my comment on stress, try to remember the following phrase, "Our level of success in life is directly proportional to our ability to embrace stress." Since we're all different and are motivated for different reasons, only you can decide what's best for you in the timing of your purchases. You will see my pattern of purchases in a subsequent chapter—it took me 11 years of buying, starting from scratch, before I reached millionaire status. Regardless of your investment goals in real estate, it's always best to see how someone else can be copied, someone who has "been there and done that." Perhaps you'll want to copy the buying pace I set for myself or choose a different pace altogether.

Before we get to some of my personal encounters on finding deals, let me address those critics who are opposed to cross-collateralizing. First of all, why would someone be opposed to a great system? Their argument is that you have to have good credit before you buy more properties. In other words, they would say you should not buy if you have damaged credit. My reaction to that is yes, eventually most people are going to need a good credit rating, which makes doing business a whole lot easier. You can restore your credit score to an acceptable level in a shorter period of time using this system, and paying on time, rather than waiting for many more years while paying on a lesser number of properties and earning less income.

On some occasions I meet people who say they never deal with banks to finance their deals, and I believe them. But why not do as I've done and improve a lower credit score to enjoy a huge luxury that I've been able to enjoy, exploding my real estate career to astronomical heights, being able to continue buying with only my signature, never having to worry about the down-payment or rehab money ever again?

Finding the Deals, or How the Deals Find You

When Good Chemistry Intervened

About 20 years ago I entered the local Savings and Loan in my hometown to make one of my many mortgage payments. In those days, paying online as is commonplace today had not been invented. Of course I could have sent the check in the mail, but, believing very strongly in person-to-person contact, I entered the Savings and Loan with my checkbook in hand. As I stepped up to the counter, the teller greeted me as I began to write out the check. As I handed it to her, she said, "Oh, Steve, there's Mr. Rathke, the bank president. Something tells me you guys would enjoy meeting each other." Then, before I knew it, we were introduced.

To make a long story short, he also had a passion for rehabbing old houses, and just like that, we became the best of friends. We even went out for lunch together every Friday for several years in a row. As he was soon to retire, over the next few years, he ended up selling me his last remaining four or five properties, including one eight-unit complex worth over $100,000. To my amazement, for three of those properties he allowed me simply to take over the payments with just my signature. Just like that, we were like a father-son combination that had finally found one another. There's always room for good chemistry in relationships, wouldn't you say?

However, if I hadn't been previously making a name for myself utilizing cross-collateralization, which allowed me to ever so quickly expand my real estate holdings and build my net worth, assuming over a quarter million dollars' worth of properties belonging to Mr. Rathke would never have been possible. He never would have heard of Steve Ames, and we certainly never would have been introduced!

When It's Who You Know

One day about 2005, as I was going about my day, my cell phone rang. It was a man named Vince from Pennsylvania who had flown to Iowa to visit a property he'd just bought on the Internet. As it turned out, the house was not the gold mine he'd expected, and he suddenly was anxious to sell. He was so anxious that he needed to find a buyer quite quickly, and catch a flight back home, all in less than 24 hours. Luckily for me, as I ended up buying the property for only $14,000, a local attorney had passed my name and phone number to the new buyer, who later that day sold it to me. Though I'd given the attorney some work previously, Vince would never have called me if it weren't for the concept of who you know.

When Acquaintances Call

This purchase took place in the late 1990s, and, like the previous deal, it too was initiated by a phone call. On the other end of the line was Leona, the aunt of a former girlfriend. After a minute or so of chitchat, she began describing an old motel that she and her husband wanted to sell. As it turned out, I bought the 15-unit motel and all the land for only $30,000—one of the best purchases I ever made. Though we hadn't seen each other in decades, this example shows that friends and acquaintances will still remember you!

When in the Right Place at the Right Time

When I visited a real estate agency to pick up a key to an empty house, where I had been hired to do some painting, there was no key to be found. In the meantime, another realtor from the same office, specializing in commercial real estate sales, decided to help. He was familiar with the house in question and decided to do a brief search for the key. As he helped chase down the missing key, he calmly said, "You should let me show you a seventeen-unit building we've had on the market awhile." As we got acquainted, he told me about how a local businessman had rashly made the purchase a few years earlier for $195,000 but soon realized owning and managing apartments was not his forte and wanted to sell. When I asked about the price, he said, "Well, it's listed for one hundred nineteen thousand five hundred, but I'm sure the owner will take less." As luck would have it, I made the purchase for $96,500, a fantastic deal, but only because I just happened to be in the right place at the right time.

When a Loan Officer Wanted to Help

While walking through the bank one day to make a deposit, I noticed my loan officer motioning me to his office. As I entered we shook hands and then he said, "Hey, Steve, I was hoping to see you one of these days." When I asked what was on his mind, he said, "We've got a house on Lee Street we want you to look at." He continued, "Our bank will just let you take over the existing mortgage, if you're interested." In this case, though the loan officer first had the interest of the bank in mind, he still very clearly wanted to help me out because of the good rapport we had with each other.

When an Old Mentor Came Calling

Several years ago my old friend and mentor, Elmer, contacted me. He said, "Steve, I want you to have that big house up on North

First Avenue." He went on, "That guy dating my daughter was going to take it, but he ain't been treating her right, and I want you to have it." Though we had a great friendship and he freely gave me tons of very valuable advice, I never once had expected even a penny as a gift from him. What a great surprise it was to receive a property worth three or four times the price I paid. Elmer sold it to me for exactly what he had just paid, perhaps in return for the utmost respect I always showed to him as my mentor.

When a Realtor Reached Out

While exchanging pleasantries on the sidewalk one day, my realtor friend Dean said to me, "Steve, why don't you go see the people at the bank up there on the corner? I was told about a couple of repos on their books that they would like to get rid of." As luck would have it, though two other repo buyers were ahead of me, each rejected a property I ended up buying, which after some basic remodeling put close to $20,000 instant equity in my pocket. However, in this case, Dean had absolutely nothing to gain, except perhaps a continued friendship. He profited not even a single penny on the deal, as he indeed could have. He just decided to reach out to me.

When My Local Bank Decided I Was the One

As the mid-1990s rolled around, I found my feet firmly planted in the rental property business. My portfolio of old bulldoze-able busted-up shacks had grown considerably, and I'd begun to accumulate duplexes, four-plexes, an eight-plex or two, and by then could even lay claim to my biggest real estate holding of all, a 17-unit apartment complex. I had even reached the milestone of being able to declare, for the first time ever, that my net worth had reached $1 million. By massaging the numbers slightly, I had indeed declared myself a millionaire and was riding a wave of good real estate deals.

Isn't it intriguing how we sometimes are appropriately recognized for this or that accomplishment, even before we've convinced ourselves that we're deserving? While making a deposit one morning, the chief loan officer and senior vice president of what used to be Security Bank in my hometown, tapped me on the shoulder and said, "Steve, we'd like to talk to you about some properties the bank is handling. Do you have a few minutes?"

The next thing I knew, I was given a list of 26 properties all confiscated by the bank from a construction company that had just gone under. Just like that I was given the chance of accepting all the properties, rejecting all the properties, or cherry-picking only those I wanted.

My first reaction was to wonder, *Could this really be happening to me?* Had I really gained that much trust and respect from bankers? I asked myself, *Am I really rubbing shoulders with those who can give me the most favorable interest rate and allow me to pay the least, if anything at all, to take control of so many properties so quickly?* The answer was yes, yes, yes! It really was true!

By the way, in case you're wondering, I cherry-picked some but rejected the vast majority. Looking back, I can't believe how stupid I was. Oh, how I wish I could turn back the clock! Obviously, I should have taken every single one of those properties. However, the message here is this: One of these days, your local bank just might decide that *you're the one*, as happened to me. In other words, good deals will sometimes find you.

Though I benefited greatly on those few deals I cherry-picked, I just hope you are more prepared than I was.

When Coffee Table Tips Are Passed

By the early 1990s, the word was circulating in my hometown of roughly 27,000 inhabitants that Steve Ames was the guy to call if an older property was being considered for sale. At that time, a local attorney had begun drinking coffee off and on with our group at least one day each week or so. After about the third or fourth visit to our coffee table, he said to me, "Steve, I'm helping a lady through her divorce, and I think she has a property you'd be interested in." I immediately said, "Absolutely. Please tell me a little more about it."

He explained how she was moving to Des Moines, about an hour away, and that she wanted nothing more to do with the property because of bad memories. Though she was awarded the property in her divorce settlement, she just wanted to dump it and get on with her life. As it turned out, it was a large lot with two separate houses. One house consisted of a medium-sized two-bedroom single-family dwelling with an attached garage. The other was a recently remodeled three-unit complex consisting of two one-bedroom apartments and one two-bedroom unit.

Though there was around $15,000 left on the mortgage of both places combined, to finish paying her legal bills, she was only asking $16,000. She wanted to have the property sell quickly to be able to put the whole thing behind her and get on with her life. The purchase of this property was perhaps the best deal of that whole decade, though all of my best coffee table tips combined would take up an entire book. I would strongly urge you to seek out or start your own group of people to get together with at a coffee shop or restaurant, to brainstorm with on a regular basis.

Swaying the Deal

Scavenging the purchase not only refers to buying properties with collateral from other properties but with little or none of your own money. It also encompasses swaying the deal, or using your influence to get better terms, a better price, or making everything about the purchase better for you, the buyer. Let me explain how swaying a deal back in the 1990s led to a fantastic purchase.

The year was 1997. When I answered the phone, a lady's voice asked, "Steve, is that you?" She continued, "This is Leona. Do you remember me?" I had dated her niece nearly 25 years earlier. She went on, "Orley and I have the old motel out on Iowa Avenue and would like to sell it." Within moments, after telling me where to find the master key, she made me promise to go by, have a look, and call her the following morning. Before we said good-bye, she said, "Steve, we've established the value at over one hundred thousand dollars, but Orley says we might consider ninety thousand."

Early the next morning, before I had a chance to call her, Leona called me again. In terms of swaying the deal, at that instant, because she called me so early the next morning, I knew she was a motivated seller. I also knew she had already started to yield to me some degree of leverage.

As we began to talk about the property, my goal was to destabilize her psyche and strongest points. I started mentioning as many deficiencies as I could, including some doors that didn't shut right, the older-style non-thermopane windows that eventually would have to be changed, the unattractive aging roof, and, among other things, the completely flooded basement that contained the boiler, both water heaters, and about five feet of water.

I knew this was the time to *downplay the niceties* and *exaggerate the deficiencies*. Be aware that *timing is everything* in being able to sway a deal. The *most opportune moment* usually rolls around only once, and you need to be ready. Let me further add, though most of you are aware, that some deals are killed because of sarcasm, the wrong choice of words, or the wrong tone of voice. Just remember that kindness goes a very long way in any form of communication or negotiation and has never been known to kill a deal.

Suddenly Leona said, "Well, Steve, what do you think, would you like to have the property?" As I began restating the deficiencies, including many *hypothetical unforeseen variables* that may have been lurking only to be revealed once the rehab was underway, she abruptly said, "Steve, Orley and I decided we could go as low as sixty thousand. Is it a deal?" At that moment I wanted to scream, "Hell, yes." However, something told me to stall a little longer, so I began mentioning the high cost of labor and materials, among other things.

Then, within a heartbeat, Leona said, "Promise me you'll sleep on it one more night and call me in the morning." On the morning of the third day, sure enough, before I barely had time to get out of bed, Leona called me again. When I answered the phone, Leona said, "Good morning, Steve. Now that you've thought about it overnight, are you ready to take the property for sixty thousand?" Though I was prepared to say yes, I first said something like, "There sure is a lot of rehab there." I hadn't even finished my sentence when Leona said, "If you bring us a signed contract by three pm today for thirty thousand, Orley says we'll let you have it!" As the phone nearly fell out of my hand, with my voice cracking, I said, "Sounds like a deal to me. I'll see you soon."

Looking back on it, another thing that worked in my favor was the fact that I never once mentioned a price. One of my mentors had told me just before that purchase, "The first person to mention a price in any form of negotiations always loses." Even though that might not be true 100% of the time, it is true the vast majority of the time, and being the first to mention a price will do nothing but hurt you in any kind of a business deal.

Getting Your Terms

Scavenging the purchase entails more than methods of buying, swaying the deal, or getting the best price. It also entails getting your terms. Let's suppose that the very best price you can obtain has been agreed upon between you and the seller and etched in stone. But what about the terms? If you have a very acceptable price but not such favorable terms, is it still a good deal?

Would you pay 25% under the market value for a property if the best interest rate you could get was a 20% fixed rate for the next 10 years?

How about this: Would you pay 25% over the current market value for a property if the interest rate were 0% for the next 10 years? Now do you see where I'm coming from? Can you now see that getting your terms in the purchase of anything is really the most important part of the transaction?

The main thing to remember is to not get caught sleeping. In other words, don't be stubborn and convince yourself that taking a contract to an attorney to be examined is not necessary. Especially if you're new at the game of buying, you will need to fully understand such concepts as balloon payments, amortization schedules, fixed rates versus variable rates of interest, and so on. Whether you're an experienced buyer or not, the consensus now and always has been to have any type of legal document examined by an attorney.

Before leaving this segment on finding the deals, and because it's such an important part of real estate, even though, as I just explained, the vast majority of my deals seemed to find me, I realize some of you just might not be as lucky as I was. Therefore, I'm going to make for you a simple list of some of the more conventional, but highly effective, ways to find your deals. Nowadays, though you can sub-scribe to monthly listings far and wide that will show you "where all the good deals are," for bankruptcies, foreclosures, defaulted mortgages, courthouse auctions, and so on, from those in your area to those list-ings nationwide, I feel you still need to know where to look for deals in your immediate area. The following is a list of places where I would look to find the most economical "scavengable" deals, where you can find attractively low prices, or where you can negotiate to make your purchase price much more attractive. Remember, if you're new at the game, as I suspect many of you are, you can't pay top-of-the-market prices and expect to win big. That's just not going to happen. To give you a small idea as to what I mean, before you buy, locate approximately 10 houses that have been considerably discounted for whatever reason in comparable neighborhoods, then negotiate the price on all of them as low as possible like there's no tomorrow. Then, among those two or three with the lowest price, decide which one will provide you the most amount of profit with the least amount of hassle. At that point you simply say, "I'm ready to sign the sales contract."

Though I just gave you a very quick lesson in how to buy, that's basically how I became successful and how I still buy my deals, even today, 37 years after having bought my first property. So, get wise and go do some deals. As we end this chapter, I leave you with this quote: "When the student is ready, the teacher will appear." Now, go make some money!

More conventional ways to find scavengable deals are through these sources:

- Realtors
- Banks
- Finance companies
- Newspaper real estate ads
- FSBO yard signs
- Craigslist
- eBay
- Online auctions
- Bankruptcy attorneys
- Management companies (for multifamily complexes)
- Property managers

Key Points

- Scavenging the purchase in this chapter refers to transferring collateral from a previously purchased property to another you're about to buy, usually using only your signature, which is a process known as cross-collateralizing or cross-collateralization.

- Your equity or collateral will continue to grow as you make improvements to your property, coupled with the rate of inflation.
- Pulling collateral from one property to purchase another also will allow you to not only satisfy the down payment, but also to utilize rehab funds made available in the same transaction.
- Using rehab funds made available by taking collateral from one property and applying them to another keeps you from having to tap into personal savings and checking accounts.
- The speed and frequency of purchases is an individual thing depending on your ability to embrace stress.
- Take up to a year to renovate your first purchase, but rent it as soon as possible, utilizing the incoming rent to pay bills and continue to modernize.
- To buy your second property with just your signature, have your first property appraised by a local bank when renovations are complete.
- Banks need customers like you to continue making loans in order to stay in business.
- A successful career in real estate may depend on the following quote, "Our level of success in life is directly proportional to our ability to embrace stress."
- Copy those who have "been there and done that."
- A low credit score is no excuse for not cross-collateralizing since it can be rebuilt rather quickly and will be necessary eventually, down the road, anyway.
- Realizing that good chemistry exists between you and someone who is able to help you can be extraordinarily helpful and may explode your property holdings and net worth.
- You'll be more successful in real estate when "who you know" greatly helps you acquire property.
- Acquaintances will remember you, sometimes decades later, giving you more favorable odds.
- Being in the right place at the right time is sometimes a contributing factor in you finding a fantastic deal.

- A bank loan officer will sometimes designate you over others, as the person approached when a good deal comes along, simply because you maintained good rapport with that person.
- An old mentor may come calling when you least expect it to inexplicably offer you a fabulous deal, perhaps in return for the utmost respect you have always showed to that mentor.
- Out of the blue, a realtor friend might reach out to offer you great advice, for unknown reasons.
- Make your presence known at your local bank and it's only a matter of time before that bank will decide to help you, giving you access to great deals, such as bankruptcies, non-performing notes, etc.
- Having a group to drink coffee with will invariably result in stellar information passed to you, resulting in great purchase(s) of real estate.
- Kindness goes a long way in any form of negotiation and has never been known to kill a deal.
- Use hypothetical unforeseen variables to get the seller to lower the asking price.
- The first person to mention a price in any form of negotiations usually loses.
- Getting your price is one thing, but the terms of the deal overshadow the price, such as if there is a balloon payment, if there is a variable or fixed rate of interest, and if the payment schedule is amortized.
- Always have any legal transaction examined by an attorney.
- Though good deals will sometimes, somehow, find you, be aware of highly effective ways to find deals.
- After narrowing your search, always decide upon the property that will provide you the most amount of profit with the least amount of hassle.
- "When the student is ready, the teacher will appear." Now, go make some money!

Three

Scavenging
the Materials

If you've already gotten this far reading this book, you understand something about the importance of utilizing scavenged materials to boost equity and increase profits. However, in this chapter, I'll give you first-hand examples of how I was able to do just that and, at the same time, will broaden your prospective by pointing out a variety of places to look to help you meet your needs.

Like my father used to say "Don't just tell me, give me the road-map, take me by the hand, and lead me to the spot! That's precisely what I hope to do in this chapter.

Deconstructors

As I comment in chapter 6, "Scavenging the Deconstruction," the quickest way to put your hands on the largest variety of recycled materials for the least amount of investment is to contact a decon-struction company or individual or go straight to the site where deconstruction is underway.

To be quite honest, the word *deconstruction* was not even a part of my vocabulary until a few years ago. But, after recently buying properties in the Houston, Texas, area and doing more research on the topic, this word quickly became engraved in my mind.

Just last year, as my search for good-quality recyclable materials broadened in the Greater Houston area, I was given the name and phone number of a well-known deconstructor, Tee, and also that of his business partner, Jay.

These two guys dedicate their whole livelihood to deconstruction, even carrying on their work as a second-generation business. In a nutshell, their business simply consists of finding a particular structure that is to be torn down. At that point they simply make contact with the old landlord, with the new landlord, or with the demolition company, depending upon the situation.

From then on, a contract is created that spells out all the terms and conditions and gives the deconstruction company the right to deconstruct before a certain deadline passes. Then, of course, after the deadline passes, cranes and bulldozers roll in, and the rest is history.

For example, a deconstructor might, in turn, form a contract with you. He might say, "OK, give me three hundred and fifty dollars per unit, but have everything you want from each apartment removed by next Saturday." He may sell you the right to scavenge 10 apartments, let's say apartments numbered 36 to 45.

As a matter of fact, this is precisely the situation I found myself in with Tee and Jay just a few months ago in Houston. They were calling landlords and apartment complex investors far and wide. They had just identified an apartment complex of roughly 600 units that was soon to be demolished to make way for commercial expansion.

Though we chose to buy only refrigerators and stoves, the option was available to me to remove everything possible from each apartment for a certain agreed-upon price.

Although most of you can imagine already what I'm about to say, let me give you an idea of some of the items I could have removed from those apartments before I move on to the next section:

> windows, doors, carpets and pads, curtains and mini blinds, upper cabinets, lower cabinets, countertops, ceiling fans, light fixtures, switches, electrical outlets, thermostats, furnaces, air conditioners, breaker panels, window trim, door trim, baseboards, washers and dryers, stoves, refrigerators, dishwashers, microwaves, fireplace mantels, bathroom vanities, mirrors, medicine cabinets, toilet stools, towel racks, mailboxes, lamp posts, etc.

As I've just indicated, getting to the site of deconstruction before the demolition and coordinating with the deconstructor to *get in and out* in the narrowest of time frames is the key. My suggestion, if you really want to *capitalize* on this for literally pennies on the dollar, would be to line up access to a large borrowed or rented truck a few days ahead of time if you don't already have one, have access to minimal storage space such as a few double garages, and have five or six part-time laborers lined up and ready to work upon short notice. Then, when the final day rolls around, before being forced to evacuate the work site, the deconstructor will almost certainly cut his price in half once, or even twice more, just to generate slightly more money from the project that he would never see otherwise.

Finally, in all my 37 years of owning properties and scavenging, if you've been looking for my most powerful message about putting your hands on the materials, this would have to be it! Sure, you can go to an auction, a total liquidation sale, or whatever and get lucky there, but in my opinion, maintaining good rapport with a deconstructor outweighs all other options! Units about to be demolished are a scavenger's one-stop shopping center.

Home Improvement Stores

Virtually every time I go to a home improvement store such as Lowe's, Menards, Home Depot, and so on, regardless of whatever else I have on my mind, I always head straight to the bargain bins. As I discussed in my first book, *Scavenge Your Way to Wealth; The Hidden Secrets That Turn Huge Profits*, some real bargains can be found from time to time in the bargain bins. However, the key words here are "from time to time." Though good-quality, though sometimes damaged, items can be found at reasonable discounts, finding what you need in large enough quantities can be a problem, not to mention always having to be there at the "most opportune moment" and "get lucky" at the same time.

But, having said all that, since most of you are only remodeling no more than one or two properties at any given time, until your business starts to grow by leaps and bounds, you shouldn't need truckloads of materials with any degree of frequency. Just continue buying from the bargain bins little by little, adding to your reserves as you go.

Since your sources of materials will be so wide-ranging and will come from many different places, the more you get used to buying piecemeal and practicing "delayed gratification," the better off you will be.

I, to this day, keep notes in my pocket on certain measurements for items I'm going to need several months from now, when I get around to remodeling a porch, a bathroom, and so on. If I accidentally find, for example, two windows of the five or so I'm going to need to complete a project a few months down the road, I simply reach into my wallet and cross them off my list each time I buy until I've located all the parts of the puzzle.

As I mention in chapter 8, "Scavenging the Expertise," create personalized watchdogs to be on the lookout for bargains whenever you can at such types of stores and you'll be well on your way to building a real estate empire.

Store Closings

Just last year the Menards store in my hometown of Marshalltown, Iowa, closed. No, they didn't go bankrupt or lose their lease on the building. They simply closed that location because they had built a new store less than a mile away.

My first reaction was that they surely would load everything up and haul it away, especially since the new store was only a stone's throw down the road. To my surprise, they hauled away not a single item of any kind! Since their date to be completely gone from the building was only four weeks away, they had a closeout sale.

On the day the new Menards store opened, I recall going into their old store just to have a look around. Since discount ads were being run in the local newspaper, I couldn't wait to get there.

As I entered the old store, I asked the first sales clerk I saw, "When did all these discounts begin?" Her response was, "Two weeks ago everything in the store was discounted twenty percent, then last week an extra twenty percent discount was added, making everything in the store forty percent off." I then asked, "What about next week?" She then said, "Until we finally close two weeks from now, everything will drop again by twenty percent, making all items in the store sixty percent off. However, beyond that, each individual department also is offering an additional discount of ten to thirty-five percent, making all merchandise seventy to ninety-five percent off the last two week of operation."

As she finished, I said, "Does that even include all those big beautiful display kitchens with granite countertops?" Her answer was, "Yes, sir, everything in the store." My scavenger-hunting spirit had led me to a true scavenger's heaven or playground.

Total Liquidation Sales

Total liquidation sales, though similar to ordinary store closings, are usually the result of bankruptcies. Chances usually increase dramatically that you'll find prices slashed to absolute minimums in a shorter period of time after the sale is first announced. Unlike other store closings where owners have planned their retirement long in advance and are not in a hurry to sell out, total liquidation sales usually start and end during a very narrow time frame, whereby the main idea is move the stock and empty out the store as quickly as possible.

I've been at some of these "everything in the store must be sold quickly" types of sales where I've witnessed a few big-time scavengers wheel and deal. They simply pull up out front with a big truck and two or three helpers, rush into the store, and quickly identify the person in charge, only to make a ridiculously lowball offer. Because they guarantee they can reduce a ton of stock at lightning speed, the store manager often feels obligated to bite and make the sale.

Hey, why not use this same tactic? What the heck, even if the store manager is too hard to deal with, you will have lost absolutely nothing except for the time it took to swing by. If he says, "Yes, you've got a deal," look at all you will have gained! Why not follow Donald Trump's advice when he says, "Since you have to think anyway, regardless of what it is, you might as well think big."

Want Ads

The want ads or classified ads in your local newspaper are another option always available to you for finding materials. On top of usually being able to find announcements for yard sales, porch sales, garage sales, and so on, one of my favorite places to look in the newspaper is the column labeled "merchandise/miscellaneous." As a matter of fact, most yard sales and garage sales come to a halt when colder weather rolls around, here in the upper Midwest, but there's always someone selling something year-round if you bother to check the merchandise column.

A few years back, there was a time when I depended heavily upon buying almost daily from the want ads to meet my need for materials to rehab my houses and apartments. At that time our local newspaper didn't become available until around one in the afternoon, so I remember driving directly to the newspaper office very frequently to get my hands on it the moment it became available. That was the only way I knew at the time to stay ahead of my competition, and, for the most part, it really did pay off.

One time I recall picking up the newspaper and finding an ad that mentioned something like, "children's toys, a bicycle, clothing, and many other odds and ends..." As I finished reading the ad, I noticed the last two words were "and cabinets." Though something seemed strange about the ad, since I was so desperate for cabinets and had time on my hands, I quickly dashed across town to get to the garage sale just before it started.

To make a long story short, the lady conducting the sale said, "I'm sure glad you came for the cabinets." She was anxious to get rid of them and clean out her utility shed. As she opened the utility shed door, she said, "Would they be worth two dollars apiece to you?" They were so numerous and in such good condition, I couldn't believe my eyes. As I hesitated momentarily before responding, she, thinking that she needed to correct herself, immediately said, "Why don't you just give me a dollar apiece for them and I'll help you load them up?"

Though I've just described one of my many successes at yard sale scavenging, nothing was unusual about it, meaning you too can create a series of similar successes in much the same way. Be consistent, be perseverant, and work hard at it. Remember, luck almost always doesn't just happen, but rather is something you yourself create by staying focused and giving your goal your full attention.

Before leaving this topic on want ads, let me leave you with a few final thoughts. One thing I used to do when I bought frequently from the ads was to buy many things I didn't even need as long as I knew I could make a killing reselling them at a later date. Many times the people were so anxious to get rid of this or that, they would say, "Why don't you do me a favor and take that thing along with you, at no charge?"

Between what I bought for 10 cents on the dollar, coupled with what I hauled away for free, I created a secondhand store. Though the business required some hustle, I always made good money. However, nowadays, if I had it all to do over again, to cut overhead expenses, I'd either hold an auction every 90 to 120 days, pay an individual a commission to conduct sales on eBay, or both. If this idea is something you haven't thought of before now, and if you really want to get ahead a little faster, then let this small bit of advice be another one of your freshly harvested mini golden nuggets as you work to scavenge your way to real estate riches.

Secondhand Stores

Another method of being able to put your hands on building materials is paying a visit to a secondhand store. As you know, these stores can be found all over and include the likes of Salvation Army thrift stores, Goodwill, and innumerable independent types. However, there are few stores in general that carry only building materials. Apart from the independent stores you find here and there, the Habitat for Humanity ReStores are a very viable option. According to the Internet, they are located in 49 of the 50 states of the United States, with many locations found within certain states.

I first heard the term "Habitat for Humanity" a few decades ago when former president Jimmy Carter was shown with a team of volunteers on television, helping build Habitat for Humanity houses for the needy.

The Habitat for Humanity ReStores function as a nonprofit entity whereby all surplus money generated goes into the building of homes for the less fortunate, such as people who have lost their homes in a flood, by fire, and so on, have no insurance, finding themselves destitute.

As you can see, this organization not only helps the needy with its profits, but also helps society by providing an outlet for rehabbers and ordinary citizens alike to purchase used building materials that otherwise might go into the landfills. Not only do Habitat for Humanity ReStores allow us a drop-off point for quality used materials we no longer wish to keep after remodeling, but they offer much more.

For example, the ReStores not only provide a place to drop off or purchase good used building materials, but they also handle brand-new building materials at discount prices. They receive shipments all the time from manufacturers that donate their new materials for various reasons. Some of those reasons include overstock of certain brands that haven't sold well, the need to clean out a particular warehouse, the discontinuing of certain makes and models of one type of merchandise or another, and so forth.

Last, it should be mentioned that the main reason why large companies donate so freely and will probably continue to do so is because of the huge federal tax breaks these companies receive in exchange for their donated materials. Perhaps we will always have good-quality building materials available to us to do our rehabs, as long as Uncle Sam continues to provide these enormous tax breaks to "rehabber's havens" such as the Habitat for Humanity ReStores.

Before moving on to discuss discount stores, in case you're just getting involved in rehabbing or are unaware, you only have to take a look around to find similar types of stores, many located nowadays in shopping malls, offering new merchandise at greatly reduced prices.

As a caution, just because the ReStores serve a very worthy cause, and get everything donated to them 100% free, doesn't mean they always have the lowest prices, as you will discover.

Discount Stores

The explosion of discount stores around the country in recent years never ceases to amaze me. In general, I remain dumbstruck at just how many discount chain stores exist—they are seemingly every-where far and wide. And what's even more amazing is the variety of products found at these stores, many times at steeply discounted prices. Even my hometown of Marshalltown, Iowa, with a population of slightly less than 30,000, has such stores as Dollar General, Dollar Tree, General Dollar, Family Dollar, and, until recently, Big Lots.

Because of these discount stores, I've been able to save tons of money on such things as pest control products, spray paints, cleaners, and less common items like toilet plungers and specific types of tools.

As I was driving by a Big Lots only yesterday, something told me to enter the store, just to have a look around, but more specifically to note all the products that would be of interest to landlords and property investors. In case you haven't been in one of these types of stores lately, have a look at the lists I compiled to see just how much these greatly discounted products can be of help to you and your business. The following lists are what I found. Note that I've divided my findings into five different categories:

General items:

- Mini blinds
- Bamboo roll-up drapes
- Garden hoses
- Ratcheted tie-down straps
- Extension cords

- Surge protectors
- Door knobs and locks
- Padlocks
- Light bulbs
- Tools (basic)
- Kitchen and bath faucets
- Shower heads
- Toilet seats
- Shower poles (curved and straight)
- Shower curtains
- Curtains
- Curtain rods (many decorative varieties)
- Mirrors
- Rugs
- Welcome mats
- Towel bars and racks
- Shelving totes

Cleaning supplies:

- Vacuum cleaners
- Brooms and mops
- Garbage can liners
- Waste baskets
- Cleaners and scratch pads (huge variety) for
    - Windows
    - Ovens
    - Floors
    - Kitchens
    - Baths

Office supplies:

- Calculators
- Staplers

- Scissors
- Magic markers
- Tape
- Envelopes
- Paper clips

Painting supplies:

- Rollers
- Roller trays
- Roller covers
- Brushes
- Caulking
- Drop clothes

Décor for staging houses and apartments:

- Vases
- Clocks
- Candle holders
- Soap dispensers (very attractive)
- Paintings
- Wall hangings
- Furniture
- False fire places

Contractors and Subcontractors

Just a few years back when I was in the "heavy thick of things," as I like to say, I was quite the person for creating lists of people who could help me. The vast majority of these people consisted of contractors and subcontractors. Not only did I keep them on my list to be able to pick their brains, but also because they turned out to be an excellent source for scavengable materials.

In the case of cabinet makers, for example, I'd always beg them to save the old sets of cabinets they would remove before installing new ones for me. Also, I'd always go out of my way to make "my involvement" in the deal as hassle free as possible for them. I would insist that they take some cash from me to try to ensure they'd always remember me on each and every future transaction. These small company contractors and subcontractors did me a world of good over the years and provided me with treasure troves of rehab materials, even though on rare occasions, to be honest, I was asked to pay a higher price for an item than its actual value.

Though I constantly raided dumpsters behind carpet stores, I also leaned heavily on the flooring installers of the community to provide me with good-quality used carpeting, among other flooring products they had access to at greatly reduced prices. These types of subcontractors not only will be able to help you directly but will also pass along to you valuable information from time to time. For example, they perhaps missed the bid on a big job—say a new store going into a shopping center—but can tell you the date the new floor is to be put down. These small bits of information can be a big help.

HVAC Dealers and Wholesalers

HVAC dealers and their wholesale distributors, combined with all types of service and installation technicians of the heating and cooling industry, have also helped me immensely over the years. They've helped by selling me "scratch and dent" new models of furnaces and air conditioners at fantastically low prices and by helping me find good used models for free.

For example, once I found a wholesale distributor in a neighboring town that had dozens of new scratch-and-dent furnaces for sale. During the following year or so, I ended up buying about a dozen of them for only 5% over manufacturer's cost. Since almost all of them were installed in the basement of rental properties, I didn't have to be the least concerned about the appearance. Not only that, but not a single one had an objectionable appearance, and only a few had minor problems, such as a cracked igniter, which costs very little to repair. By the way, there was one other thing that might catch you by surprise. Believe it or not, they gave me a full warranty on each of the new "scratch and dent" models I received!

As far as good used furnaces or air conditioners are concerned, any service or installation technician coast to coast will tell you that the majority of the older models replaced by new ones run just fine. It's just that, in many cases, people think they need to install the very latest models, sometimes only to gain 3% or 4% more efficiency, though possibly enhanced at times by manufacturer's rebates.

Many 90% to 92% efficient furnaces that run perfectly well, for example, are replaced without rhyme nor reason, at least from a con-servative's point of view, by models of perhaps 96% efficiency. Simply befriend a few installation or service technicians and your supply will never dwindle.

Going back 20 years or so, I recall being desperate for used higher efficiency furnaces. As luck would have it, my old friend and mentor, Bob, seemed to appear out of nowhere. I remem-ber running up to him, saying, "Bob, can you tell me where I can get a good used furnace or two?" He immediately said, "Steve, go to the dealer up in the north end of town." He went on, "Just pull around to the back of that building on the right where the installers pile up the older models when they return for the day."

That small bit of advice put thousands of dollars into my pockets and into my bank account. Why not let this advice be a huge golden nugget for you as it was for me?

Appliance Stores

You will also be able to find some great deals at appliance stores, both those that handle all new products, as well as the stores that handle only used items, though, as most of you have probably discovered, most appliance stores handle new and used models.

The key to buying at appliance stores is getting to know the owners well. As with all companies, once you establish good rapport with representatives, you'll begin to see the advantages. For example, many of these store owners will buy dozens to a few hundred appliances at one time. If you are a steady customer and can buy in bunches, good deals will generally come your way. In my case, the number 10 has usually been the deciding factor. In other words, if I'm able to buy at any one time 10 electric or gas stoves, 10 dishwashers, 10 window or wall air conditioners, 10 refrigerators, or a combination thereof, I've received my best deals. These owners buy good used models from corporate managers of large apartment complexes, senior citizen housing, and so on every seven years or so. If they see that they can depend on you to buy in quantity, you will be on their list, and steep discounts will soon await you.

Even buying only one or two models at a time, the more they see you in their store, considerable discounts will be forthcoming, though introducing to them your best arm-twisting techniques may have to be called upon from time to time. By the way, if employing any form of arm-twisting techniques is not your cup of tea, my best advice is to practice and make it a part of you if you are to survive in business. Since we constantly have to defend ourselves anyway, why not try to be the best negotiator you can be when the occasion arises?

Scavenging Your Own Storage Facilities

Assuming you've been in the real estate business for a while and have rehabbed a few different places, a valuable resource that's often overlooked is your own storage facilities. As we all know, it's so easy to accumulate odds and ends of building materials, but much more difficult to organize and classify them. If you're like a lot of us, you've got leftover rehab materials in three or four locations and, in some places, buried so deep you don't even know where to begin to look.

Buying ahead of time and accumulating reserves of basic rehab materials, when you can find them at practically giveaway prices, will do great wonders to your finances. However, not being able to find what you have, when you need it, can be very frustrating and detrimental to your business.

Why not make it a point to be better organized, as I finally had to conclude? Though it's very time-consuming to have to go back through all you have in reserves, the extra time will be well spent, and you'll be glad you did.

Just hire a few high school students a few Saturdays in a row, and put them to work. Your results will be amazing, and you will have paid out very little to have accomplished this task.

One thing that has really helped me be better organized is to have a measuring tape, a ballpoint pen, a notebook, and a roll of adhesive tape at each of my storage facilities. There's nothing better than to have everything organized into piles or stacks, and then labeled with the number of boxes, bundles, crates, or rolls of this or that, measurements, square footage, the age or date of purchase, and so on.

Buying at giveaway prices and maintaining reserves is absolute if you're to do well in this business. Why not let this small bit of info be yet another golden egg for you, as it always has been for me?

As this chapter on scavenging the materials draws to a close, I realize there are many other very good ways to obtain scavenged materials that I haven't listed, such as through auctions, estate sales, truckload sales, and so forth. However, the information in this chapter was what I was most familiar with and should serve the majority of you quite well. Perhaps with the help of some of you, by the time this book is reprinted, I will be able to include more universal and beneficial information on scavenging the materials.

Key Points

- Use the resources you already have rather than new ones whenever possible.
- Increase your equity through planned renovations.
- Buy items that are in pristine, used condition or new items that are merely damaged, discontinued, discolored, etc.
- Yard sales, garage sales, secondhand stores, friends, and the miscellaneous columns in newspapers are great sources for discounted materials.
- Store closings are another effective way to obtain high-quality items at steep discounts. The deals will be ripe for picking just prior to the store closing permanently.
- Bargain bins contain both closeout items and damaged items, both of which you can use.
- Locations that can contain a variety of materials may not have what you're looking for at a particular time. Sometimes you need to go to a specialized store or other location to find a specific type of material.
- Independent contractors who install kitchen cabinets may let you buy old cabinets that their customers didn't want.
- A cheaper way to buy materials without sacrificing overall quality is to purchase scratch-and-dent items.
- Wholesale stores are an easy way to buy low-cost appliances.
- Furnace installation businesses throw away leftover, perfectly good furnaces you can scavenge.
- If possible, buy used appliances from an area that has an overabundant supply.

- Always take into account the quantity you need in deciding where to buy appliances.
- Organize what you have salvaged so you can use it to your financial advantage.

Four

Scavenging the Labor

The idea of "scavenged labor" first became firmly implanted in my mind when I was a mere child. The year was 1959. My dad had invited a middle-aged man, Les, to live with us. Les couldn't read, write, or drive a vehicle of any kind, but he was very likable and had great manual skills. He had accepted my dad's offer of one dollar per day, with room, board, and washing, and ended up staying with us for a month or two at different times during the year.

Many years later, when I was in my twenties, the idea had really stuck, and I found myself employing scavenged laborers in my contract painting business and in my rental property business that soon followed.

So what really is scavenged labor? I define it as the process of finding and employing certain individuals or groups of individuals to your financial benefit, allowing you to avoid paying what I call *union-scale wages* for the same tasks that can be performed often for approximately two or three times less money, if not sometimes for free. Though the following list may seem detailed to some of you, I'm quite sure that many more examples could be added to it. Even though I will comment only briefly on some of these categories of scavenged labor to keep this chapter at a reasonable length, each apply or have applied to me in my life, either briefly, directly, or indirectly. They will eventually allow you, also, to scavenge your way to real estate riches and contribute to the betterment of society by offering employment to many who otherwise would have a much bleaker existence.

Categories of scavengable labor:

- Journeymen, helpers, assistants, and/or self-employed plumbers
- Journeymen, helpers, assistants, and/or self-employed electricians
- Journeymen, helpers, assistants, and/or self-employed technicians
- Journeymen, helpers, assistants, and/or self-employed gas fitters
- Journeymen, helpers, assistants, and/or self-employed carpenters
- Journeymen, helpers, assistants, and/or self-employed cabinet makers
- Journeymen, helpers, assistants, and/or self-employed block layers
- Journeymen, helpers, assistants, and/or self-employed flooring installers
- Journeymen, helpers, assistants, and/or self-employed appliance repairmen
- Journeymen, helpers, assistants, and/or self-employed landscaping contractors
- Journeymen, helpers, assistants, and/or self-employed subcontractors
- Journeymen, helpers, assistants, and/or self-employed HVAC contractors
- Journeymen, helpers, assistants, and/or self-employed cement contractors
- Journeymen, helpers, assistants, and/or self-employed paving contractors
- Journeymen, helpers, assistants, and/or self-employed seal coating and striping contractors

- Journeymen, helpers, assistants, and/or self-employed doors, windows, and siding contractors
- Tradesmen of all kinds
- The mentally challenged
- The physically challenged
- The unemployed
- The retired
- The semiretired
- The "partly disabled"
- The "fully disabled"
- Part-time workers
- Per diem/cash laborers
- Trainees
- Skill traders/barterers
- Service club members
- Church members
- Real Estate Investors Association(REIA) members
- Family
- Friends
- Acquaintances
- Neighbors
- Tavern dwellers
- Homeless shelter dwellers
- Halfway house parolees/felons
- Fire fighters
- Teachers
- Preachers
- Members of certain religious sects
- Current drug and alcohol addicts
- Recovering drug and alcohol addicts
- Immigrants
- Refugees
- Students
- Community service detainees
- Outsourced labor

In employing scavenged laborers, my secret is always to hire the person with the greatest amount of skill, with the least amount of overhead, who will accept the least amount of pay. One way to do that is to hire the "one man band" tradesmen or their helpers, assistants, or journeymen with very few exceptions. And, even for the exceptions, you can still find high-quality scavengable labor.

One exception, for example, would be if you had a massive water or gas leak, which is precisely what I had recently at my 15-unit complex.

My brother had just told me about a member of his church who had just received his master plumbers license and was looking for work. After a brief conversation with the man, I could tell he was hungry, needed work, and could operate an excavator. Water had begun to bubble up through the ground, and after the condition being reported to the water department without my knowledge, I was given just five days to fix the problem.

When it was all said and done, after having begged the city water department for an extension of a few days, I found a licensed self-employed master plumber who was willing to go to great lengths to get the job and do it perfectly, scavenging his own labor as an excavator operator, as well as that of his brother-in-law and a part-time journeyman, slashing the normal cost of the job by about one-third.

To make a long story short, after quickly getting other bids from area plumbers, this man was able to save me almost $1,500 on a roughly $5,000 job. To cut the price and assure himself he'd get the bid, this plumber, needing experienced help, called upon his own brother-in-law, who had some plumbing experience, an unemployed journeyman from where he worked, before going out on his own, plus scavenging his own expertise as an excavator operator to get the job done. This eliminated the huge cost of bringing to the job site an extra person to run the excavator had he not been blessed with this additional skill.

Before continuing, I'd like to encourage all of you to believe that high-quality scavengable labor always exists and is almost always within a stone's throw of where you are. You simply have to ask around and filter through your contacts. Even though I've just given you a personal example pertaining to plumbing, as most of you already know, the same mind-set of utilizing scavenged labor can be applied to virtually all types of scavengable task masters who can help you do flooring, roofing, landscaping, and so on.

Though these next two stories combined into one also involve plumbing and the use of an excavator, I include them here because the lessons learned were so meaningful to me and should be for you as well.

About 20 years ago, I bought an apartment complex. Soon afterward I rehabbed it and filled it with tenants. The next thing I knew, the phone rang, and I found out that the city of Marshalltown was very displeased with me. I was given 48 hours to fix a problem I knew nothing about or would be forced to move all my tenants into motel rooms and pay their expenses until the problem was completely behind me. The land owner of the property behind mine, all in a flash, had bulldozed two old Victorian-style mansions to locate his new business, breaking the main sewer line being shared by our two properties. Unfortunately raw sewage spewed across his property, onto a public sidewalk, and into the street.

After quickly assessing the situation, I called the city official back, declaring that my neighbor was 100% at fault, not me! His response was, "But the sewage is coming from your property, making you, Mr. Ames, 100% responsible for the problem it's causing."

I was barely in my early forties, having just gotten back into real estate investing after nearly a 10-year hiatus to raise my kids and go to graduate school. In other words, I had let my guard down during that 10-year hiatus, which damaged my natural defenses as a true business-man. I immediately ran to the nearest plumbing shop down the hill from the property, where I had been treated fairly on a few smaller plumbing jobs earlier that year.

The only logical way to fix "my problem" was to bring in a backhoe or excavator, dig a trench along one side of my property, and route the new sewer line the other direction toward the front of my property.

I very hastily entered the front door of the plumbing shop, "spilling my guts" to the owner, displaying complete vulnerability about the situation, as anxious and frustrated as I was, leaving myself wide open to be *taken advantage of* financially. And getting "taken advantage of" was exactly what happened to me, although it could have been avoided had I given it a tiny bit of thought or called upon a mentor (unfortunately, I had none at that time) for some simple advice.

Looking back on it, I didn't even ask the plumber for a bid. My first question to him was, "How soon can you get started on it, since we only have two days to be able to show the city that the work has begun?" That first call to me from the city official was at midmorning on a Thursday. If I'd used my head wisely, looking back on it, I had plenty of time to get three or four other bids, most probably coming close to cutting the bill in half.

As a result, I was charged $5,000 plus tax and materials. This all happened about the year 1990. This "hard-earned lesson" was so painful that I made sure it would never happen to me again. Incidentally, that plumber agreed to take payments from me for three years, allowing me to skip three months each year, January, February, and March, because of my decrease in income from my contract painting business during the winter. However, he went back on his word and threatened to take me to small claims court if the payment didn't stay the same month to month. Not only had I suffered a "setback," but also a "kick in the guts"—psychologically speaking, of course.

Now, let's fast-forward about 10 years. All of a sudden, at a different property, I found myself with roughly the same scenario: needing to dig a ditch approximately the same width and length to replace a broken water line, costing me the same for materials as the PVC sewer lines I'd run 10 years earlier to create a new drain.

Needless to say, still feeling the financial sting from 10 ten years earlier, I immediately began to *solicit my contacts*, with a guarded mind-set of high alertness. After a few hours, I had a plan in place that was second to none. I'd found an excavator who could drive his backhoe into Marshalltown from his village 20 miles away. I had also found a plumber from a new start-up company to run the new water line after the trench was complete.

As it turned out, the plumber and excavator had coordinated everything perfectly, starting early in the day and finishing late, all in the same day. As I recall, the entire operation, including paying for material, paying the plumber's wages and the cost of the permit, and compensating the excavator, which included a separate hourly rate to drive the backhoe to and from his village, was only $480. *Did you hear that?* I negotiated the same kind of job and amount of labor 10 years later, in the same town, for 10 times less money!

Before we move on, the main lesson here, even though there are many, is, of course, that if you use your head and show patience and don't panic, very high-quality scavenged labor is available everywhere, whether it be plumbing or whatever task you need to complete.

From here to the end of the chapter, though I could write an entire book on scavenged labor, I will choose only some of the most specific examples involving my personal experiences to focus on—those that are the most compelling.

Refugees

Going back to the 1980s, even at a time when my real estate investing career was barely off the ground, I felt a strong need to hire people who needed a second chance in life. During that time I helped sponsor two refugees from communist countries: one from Cuba, the other from Poland. Though they stayed with me only one to two years, which is probably fairly typical of most refugees before moving on, they each gained a strong foothold in American culture, which paid huge dividends for both their future and my financial enterprise.

As far as them helping me, they were always punctual and eager to go to work each day and did virtually everything I asked of them. In other words, they weren't complainers, not in any way, shape, or form. What's more, they never asked for special privileges, like needing an extended lunch hour to do this or that, and never demanded from me such things as paid holidays, health insurance, travel time pay between job sites, and other "rights" and "privileges" that our entitlement-minded society has shifted toward in recent years. They also helped me by accepting minimum wage salaries, which greatly aided me in my contract painting business. As luck would have it, the immigrant from Poland had been a painter. Not only did he have years of experience, but he had been a self-employed paint contractor in Poland just prior to coming to America. This makes such an employee far more valuable from a scavenging labor point of view.

Though the guy from Cuba didn't catch on so quickly, his dedication to the task and his loyalty to me also made him overwhelmingly valuable.

As far as me helping them, since I had already been a long-time social science teacher, as well as a teacher of a foreign language (Spanish), I was greatly able to help them hone their language skills in English, as well as in countless other ways, such as establishing savings and checking accounts, finding refugees from their home countries to help ease their transition to America, and so on.

Firemen

Your local fire department is another place to find good-quality scavengable labor. Going back several years, when I was buying and rehabbing properties fast and furiously, I hired firemen to help me on occasion. Since they work 24 hours on and 48 hours off, the majority of them work at other jobs during their time away from firefighting, and many had a variety of skills that played directly into my hand. During one four- to five-year time frame, I recall hiring about a half dozen firemen off and on to help me with such tasks as constructing new interior walls, hanging siding, putting in new windows and doors, installing cabinets and countertops, and so on. They all seemed very disciplined and responsible.

As far as their pay was concerned, the wages they requested were always very reasonable, only about 25% to 50% more than minimum wage at that time.

Members of Certain Religious Sects

A few years ago, in 2010, I bought an apartment complex in Des Moines, Iowa, of roughly 70 units. Though the place was suffering from "deferred maintenance," it was a great buy. One of the first tasks was to immediately begin taking bids from roofing contractors since water was coming through into two or three upstairs apartments each time it rained. I collected five or six bids, including a couple from scavenged laborers I thought just might do a good job at the most reasonable price. I was ready to sit down to work the phone lines to create a round-robin bidding war by phone, as I always do when big-time bucks are at stake. The very next day, I decided that enough time had passed, and by the end of that day, I intended to have the designated roofer decided upon. Late that afternoon after filtering through all the roofing bids, I had found my man, so I thought, and began to reach for the phone to make my final call of the day.

At that very moment, while grasping the phone to initiate the call, it rang. On the other end of the line I heard the voice of a child, who said, "Hey, mister, do you own apartments near the state capital, cuz dad knows roofing and noticed you need a roof?" To make a very long story short, the father called me later in the day, and the rest is history. For the lowest price on earth and the greatest amount of attention to detail I'd ever seen, the father of the boy and about 10 other friends and family members all showed up, in their long beards, straw hats, and old-fashioned shirts and pants with suspenders. They, being Amish, explained their unusual appearance, and though they all spoke German among themselves, their character and workmanship was superior, to say the least. As it turned out, they not only did the roofing, but ended up siding three sides of one three-story building on the site, as well as helping me with other tasks, all for the lowest wages I'd ever seen.

Per Diem/Cash Laborers

The concept of utilizing per diem laborers never resonated so strongly with me as it did in Houston, Texas, a few years ago, just after purchasing a property there. As I pulled up to the nearest Home Depot to run materials or be the "go-fer" for my employees at one of the apartment complexes, I noticed several dozen men crowded around the entrance and around the exit. My reaction was, *Wow, why are there so many people just standing around? Is there a march or a protest of some kind going on?*

As I parked my car and walked toward the main entrance, four or five men began to approach me, all at the same time. Within a moment I could see that many of the men were Hispanic. The first one hollered, "Habla español?" Since I speak Spanish fluently, I responded in Spanish and said, "What's going on, man?" Immediately, they all converged upon me, begging me to give them work without even asking if I might be looking for a specific form of help.

As the days went by, it was always the same scene, each time I visited that Home Depot or any other. As it turned out, we ended up employing a few of those guys here and there, from time to time, mainly for simple manual tasks at minimum-wage pay, though, as we soon discovered, some were very skilled at their crafts, looking for long-term work and willing to accept a very reasonable rate of pay, at least to start. The only negative I could see was that most wanted to be paid in cash, which, without it being recorded, as we all know, disallows any chance to show it as a deduction at income tax time.

Halfway House Parolees

Going back to the early 1990s, when I began to rent to halfway house parolees, the idea first occurred to me that these people would be an excellent source of scavenged labor. Almost from day one, as they became my tenants, they began to ask me for work. Back at that time and even now, all these people are encouraged to find employment of any kind, both full-time and part-time.

As I began to hire them, I could see many advantages in doing so, not only in terms of their abilities, but also because of the very strict rules they needed to follow while still being detained. For example, almost all were willing to accept any form of part-time work just to be able to spend as much time away from their detention facility as possible, including working for a bare minimum wage, regardless of how skilled they were in one area or the other.

Many of those who worked full-time someplace else were willing to work for me a few hours each day, either just before starting or finishing their full-time job.

So, if they worked four in the afternoon to midnight at a local factory, they might work for me from around nine in the morning to about two in the afternoon. Likewise, if their local factory shift began at midnight and continued to eight in the morning, they would either work for me beginning around nine in the morning to about one in the afternoon or, after they slept, from about three in the afternoon for two or three hours or so.

The more I hired these detainees, the more I became aware of the very wide range of skills and talents these people possessed. Though these part-time jobs were a means to an end for these people for a few weeks to a few months, they were a terrific source of salvageable labor for me.

The "Partly" and "Totally" Disabled

When I began renting my own properties starting in the 1970s, I immediately became much more aware of the numbers of people in this country who receive financial assistance of some kind. Though many of these people were very obviously physically or mentally challenged, many others who received disability checks each month appeared to be either slightly handicapped or not at all.

The more I investigated the individual cases, the more I found that many of these people really wanted to work a certain number of hours per week, and most were legally able to do so. Though some worried about losing their benefits if caught working, the vast majority could legally earn several thousands of dollars a year, up to a certain dollar amount, without being penalized or having their benefits halted.

Over the years, as these "disabled" people became my tenants, I began to hire them on a regular basis. Though the majority worked for me only a few hours here and there at minimum wage, doing basic jobs such as cleaning and painting apartments, on occasion one with considerable manual skills would surface.

One day the phone rang out of the blue, and the voice said, "Are you looking for anyone to help you fix up your properties?"

As I started to say no, I remembered a house I'd just purchased that needed siding and said, "Ah, yes, as a matter of fact, I need someone to help me side a house." The man very abruptly said, "I can do that for you."

To make a long story short, the man had just begun to receive disability payments from Social Security and wanted to stay busy doing something. Though I don't remember what I paid him, the rate of pay he'd asked was quite reasonable. Just on that one siding job alone, I saved a couple thousand dollars, about half of what it would have cost me had I hired a siding company or even a single individual doing siding for a living.

Lastly, one other important thing to keep in mind is that once you begin to hire people on disability, the word will get around very quickly, and, since many seem to associate with others who are disabled, your casual labor supply will always be ongoing.

Key Points

- Scavenged, nonprofessional labor allows you to hire the most talented people for the lowest cost.
- Find quality workers and give people a second chance by hiring people you meet at taverns or from homeless shelters and local halfway houses.
- Hire a few more workers than you need so that you always have backup workers if one individual doesn't show up.
- Non-standard pools of labor can be utilized to get the job done much cheaper
- Newly licensed professional labor, looking to get experience, and a good word of mouth reputation may give you much discounted rates.
- Try to never be in a situation where you need to hire a contractor you've never worked with before to complete an emergency repair, or the rates could be astronomical.

- Foreign labor, people looking for side jobs, and other non-traditional labor can do work for much cheaper than others if you can work around the limitation of language, availability times, and other restrictions.
- Partially disabled persons, recovering addicts, and halfway house people may require some extra supervision, they might not always be on time, but they can still do good work, and make up for any extra hassle by their much cheaper labor rates.

Five

Scavenging
the Game Plan

Now that you have learned about the various things to scavenge and ways to scavenge that I advocate in this book to be success-ful in real estate investing and rehabbing, you are now ready to carve out, conjure up, or scavenge your own road map or game plan.

Depending on your goals starting out, some of you will decide to stick with your day job, pursuing real estate investing as a hobby to produce only supplemental income. However, many more of you will undertake to make this business your career or life's calling, as I chose to do, and will need a game plan.

As with anything, the quicker you can shorten the learning curve, the better off you'll be, right? Conversely, as the old saying goes, "If you don't know where you're going, you ain't never gonna get there." Therefore, I've decided to make available to you the game plan that I eventually followed to help shorten your learning curve. But, before introducing the game plan I followed, let me offer some related thoughts that may be helpful.

Because I had "less than nothing" when I was growing up, coupled with the fact that my dad never once gave me spending money, I had always dreamed of someday becoming a millionaire. Though I didn't know how long it would take, even as a young man, because of my strong work ethic and drive, I somehow knew I had a good shot at it someday. My only problem then was finding a mentor, someone who had "been there and done that." Years went by and I still couldn't find anyone who could answer the question, "How long does it take to become a millionaire?" Like driving from New York to Las Angeles, averaging 60 mph for each mile driven, I wanted an answer—I simply wanted to know how long it would take!

Then one day I thought back on all the people who had asked me, "Steve, how long will it take me to speak Spanish?" and the way I answered them. I knew at that moment that if I could quantify a similar type of answer for people wanting to learn Spanish, then an answer had to exist for wanting to know how long it would take to become a millionaire. Even if you're not interested in learning Spanish, please allow me to briefly explain what my response was, and still is, to all those curiosity seekers.

After hearing the question, I always say the first step is to have a burning desire to learn. Then, assuming you know nothing about Spanish or any other foreign language, and you're a person of average intelligence, you need to study the language for about two semesters in a classroom setting to really understand the basic language structure. That of course will familiarize you with creating sentences, learning common verbs and their conjugations, pronunciation, frequently used nouns and adjectives, and so on. At that point, with your burning desire continuing, of course, you need to put yourself in a situation to be able to practice speaking the language many times daily, with as many native speakers as possible. Now, what I'm about to tell you makes you realize just how big a sacrifice you have to make to become relatively fluent in the language. This is usually what separates the men from the boys.

So, one year after starting to study Spanish, you'll be able to speak it, but only in an elementary sort of way. Then, after another whole year, you should be able to speak the language like a fourth grader. At the end of the third year, you'll be getting considerably better, but don't despair—your speaking skills will definitely increase, but only to the level of that of an eighth or ninth grader. Then, if you continue pursuing your language-speaking skills for two more years—or, in other words, at the end of five years—you might be able, never losing the burning desire, to express yourself similar to the average high school graduate, though it's unlikely you'll lose your accent.

There, now I've just given you a road map or game plan for becoming relatively fluent in Spanish. Since I myself am one of those who has been there and done that, doesn't that make my flesh-and-blood experience credible? Then why aren't there more people out there willing to stick their neck out and give a similar type of response when the question is asked, "How long does it take to become a millionaire?"

Because I was very disillusioned for so long, and never really found anyone who could explain it to me, it is important that I, here and now, answer that question for you. Though none of us are exactly alike, in my opinion, if you follow the steps that I followed in a similar way, then most of you should be able to produce relatively the same results. Before I show you the steps I followed, because of the controversial nature of this topic, I realize what I just said may leave me as a bigger target for criticism. However, since life has a way of making us thicker skinned as we get older, I'll welcome any lambasting I receive on this topic. Besides, since I became completely fluent in a foreign language, never having studied before the age of 26 (starting from scratch), and since I became a millionaire (starting from scratch) with no monetary help from anyone, something tells me I just might be the person qualified enough to elaborate on either topic.

Now, let's get to the game plan, as I prefer to call it. The following will give you a very clear idea as to how you, too, can watch your assets exceed your liabilities—by making key purchases, of course—allowing you to reach millionaire status on the 11th year after starting to invest. If you follow a game plan similar to the one I followed, I'm confident you should be able to achieve what I was able to achieve.

At this moment, I'm sure there is still a certain percentage of you who are thinking, "I'm not so sure about that." To that, let me just say this. Once you commit yourself and set your mind to reaching a certain goal, you'll realize many things you never dreamed of are possible, and the good deals will start to show themselves to you.

I know that might sound strange if you're just getting started in business, but it's actually true! As the old saying goes, "When the student is ready, the teacher will appear." In other words, at that point, once you're very committed—and by the way, this applies to anything—the answers will start to "jump out of the woodwork" at you, and the best purchases available, in your price range and in your area, and in the way you find it best to swing a deal, will all fall in your lap. Please believe me! No, I don't have any supernatural powers, and I've never been touched by an angel. However, I have experienced what I just said, which also is a commonly known fact, if you take the time to investigate.

As I've already mentioned, it took me many years, about 11 years all together, to become a millionaire, excluding my 9-year hiatus from investing. Let me lay it out for you, year by year.

Game Plan Number One

Year 1   Bought my first property, a single-family dwelling, with $5,500 saved from my part-time painting business

Year 2   Bought a three-plex, quickly converted it to five rental units, with equity from my first property, plus one year inflation

Year 3   Bought the four-plex next door with the new equity just created by converting the three-plex into five units; bought another single-family dwelling and paid the down payment with the bank's rehab money, made available on actual possession date

Year 4   After a nine-year hiatus, bought a four-plex for only $200, then quickly converted it to eight units

Year 5   Bought a three-plex and a two-bedroom house, both in the same purchase, using collateral from my recently converted eight-plex

Year 6   Bought a 17-unit apartment complex on contract the following year, paying 10% down with insurance money received from the fire damage of another property

Years 7–11 Bought about 10 more properties during this time, including two four-plexes side by side, paying $15,000 for both and only $1,500 for the down payment; also purchased a 15-unit apartment complex, an eight-unit complex, a five-unit complex, a three-plex, a duplex, and a few other properties, mainly single-family dwellings, all by utilizing collateral from previous purchases through cross-collateralizing loans

Now that you have the game plan I followed to become a millionaire, meaning when all my liabilities subtracted from all my assets totaled up to or slightly exceeded $1,000,000, let me tweak your enthusiasm a little more.

Because I also had a game plan to someday reach a yearly increase in net worth, or a yearly increment in assets, by $1,000,000 and was able to achieve that, let me give you that game plan as evidence that it can be done. This also makes you aware of an additional goal that you too can achieve. As I tell most everyone, once you have the determination and adopt the proper mind-set, "If I can do it, you can too!"

Game Plan Number Two

By the end of year 11, I had accumulated more than 20 properties totaling 90 to 95 rental units, which led me to one more game plan, game plan number two, that I almost overlooked, and a very important one at that. Over the next 10 to 11 years, my game plan during that time was to build equity in my properties as quickly as possible through renovations and by paying off all my mortgages, which is what I did.

About halfway through that 10- to 11-year period, I recall walking through the bank one day to make a deposit. The next thing I knew, one of the loan officers hollered, "Hey, Steve, come and see me before you leave." Within moments I found myself being offered the lowest interest rate I'd ever seen in commercial property lending, plus a chance to combine at least a dozen mortgages, which were all the properties I still didn't have paid off, reducing my many individual monthly payments down to just one monthly payment, setting up the new note to pay off in just five years.

That little moment in the bank that day offered me the opportunity to build equity ever so quickly by very aggressively eliminating so much debt in such a short period of time. That being said, it allowed me to embark on an additional game plan, the biggest and boldest of all the game plans I'd ever made in my life and one I'd never dreamed possible only a few years earlier. That third and final game plan, which greatly increased my knowledge about investing and sent my self-confidence into the stratosphere, is what I'm about to share with you.

Though I was able to explain game plan number two relatively concisely, don't overlook the huge impact it had on me! I almost certainly would not have been able to invest so aggressively in multifamily complexes, as you're about to see, in game plan number three if it weren't for consolidating so many loans when I did and paying off so much debt so quickly at a very favorable interest rate. In other words, always be looking for ways to do the same. Consolidating debt at a very favorable interest rate is always a good thing, not to mention the other benefits that come along with such a maneuver—such as aggressively paying down your debt in the short-term, as long as you have the income to do so. Soon you will be able to qualify for much larger loans, as I'm about to reveal, and instill a greater level of confidence in you from your bank's loan officers.

Game Plan Number Three

Up to this point, I knew that over-leveraging my collateral and stretching my equity to the hilt as I've always done would do wonders, but I still didn't realize just how big of an impact I could create. Numbers game or not, I still couldn't.

In 2008, just as I was about to make my final two or three payments on that five-year consolidation loan, leaving me completely debt free with 100% of all real estate paid off, I abruptly began to contemplate a change of course. I thought, should I stop now at the age of 57, call it quits, and do nothing more to challenge myself from now to the end of my life, except to collect rents and consider myself retired, or should I go for a bigger trophy? After all, a few hundred thousand dollars in yearly net income was nothing to sneeze at! However, I also knew that I still loved to make deals and couldn't stop reminding myself of the large multifamily complexes I'd always dreamed of possessing. At that moment I couldn't stop telling myself just how unhappy I'd be if I didn't use some of my equity to buy at least one large multifamily apartment complex, even if I didn't make other investments in real estate ever again.

Within days of contemplating such a decision, knowing only one purchase would more than double my income, and more than

double my entire portfolio of rental units, I succumbed to the temptation. While still trying to brainstorm all the ramifications, I soon
discovered a 108-unit complex in Des Moines listed in the *Sunday
Register*. That complex turned out to be the first of five consecutive
multifamily complex purchases in five consecutive years, starting in
2008 and ending in 2012.

To be brutally honest, buying that 108-unit complex was a big step
for me. Not to be too critical of the people back in my little beloved
village in north central Iowa, but I was still haunted by the small-town
mind-set. For example, a few years earlier, upon buying a building on
Main Street in a town just 20-plus minutes away, I was still receiving
comments like, "Gosh, Steve, did you buy that whole building?"

Ok, so just how big of an impact was I able to create? In a nutshell, the equity I was able to amass from 1997 to 2008, by way of
rapidly paying down debt, combined with appreciation and making
renovations, turned out to be a godsend. Simply put, that equity,
combined with making savvy purchases of five large multifamily complexes, one each year for five consecutive years, propelled me to
realize my third and final game plan, resulting in a yearly net worth
increment of roughly $1,000,000.

Let me also add that my yearly net worth increment of $1,000,000
just referred to does not reflect the profit each of these five complexes produce. That $1,000,000 net worth increment only reflects
the yearly reduction of mortgage balances plus a 4% to 4.5% annually anticipated appreciation rate.

For example, one of my properties of more than 100 units, located
in Texas, is worth about $3,100,000. On that property, the monthly
principal reduction, or the rate at which the mortgage reduces, is
$7,000, or $84.000 annually. However, at an annually anticipated
appreciation rate of 4.5%, or $139,500, the annual increase in value
of the property becomes $84,000 plus $139,500, for a whopping

annual increase in value of $223,500. And that's only one of the five properties purchased between 2008 and 2012 to which I refer.

Though we've not seen a lot of measurable appreciation through-out the United States in recent years, it has been noteworthy in certain areas, such as in the Houston, Texas, area where I have two properties, and if predictions are correct, higher appreciation rates are soon to be upon us everywhere. I only hope that you too will be the owner of a few larger properties, to be able to cash in, either by raising rents, by pulling equity out to buy more property, or by pock-eting a boatload of cash you will have gained through appreciation, should you decide to sell.

While we're talking about property value increases and calculat-ing rates of appreciation, let me divulge a statistic that has helped me tremendously over the years. If you're unaware, in the United States, going back a ways in history, the following three bits of infor-mation have generally held true:

- Properties in the poorer parts of town have risen at around a 4% appreciation rate over the past 100 years.
- Properties in the average parts of town have risen at around a 5% appreciation rate over the past 100 years.
- Properties in the better parts of town have risen at around a 6% appreciation rate over the past 100 years.

If you're prone to looking down the road and into the future, like I've always been, these three amazing little bits of information should be helpful.

Though the five multifamily purchases between 2008 and 2012 plunged me into debt by more than $10,000,000, I never took my eye off the prize, never once losing focus of my bigger goal. Key buys and key improvements, coupled with some appreciation, have already pushed upward the total combined value of these properties to an amount that exceeds $15,000,000, all in slightly less than five years.

Now the question is, how many of you would have quit after plan two, being satisfied with an income of only a few hundred thousand dollars per year, and done nothing more? And how many of you would have gone for the bigger trophy, like I chose to do, and bought the five properties, to be able to watch your net worth increase by a minimum of $1,000,000 per year (on automatic pilot)?

Regardless of your response, let me reiterate that finding a mentor is so very crucial to your success in so many ways. Whether you follow one or all three of my game plans or those of someone else, always have someone with experience who you can trust close by, someone who has been there and done that. You will be glad you did. At the very least join a REIA (Real Estate Investors Association) in your area. I also will have one-on-one counseling, group coaching, and mastermind groups you'll be able to join. Please check my website at *www.scavengeyourwaytowealth.com* or *www.scavenger-central.com* for more information.

In conclusion to scavenging the game plan, if you've gotten this far in reading this book, you probably are a serious investor and rehabber of investment properties. Therefore, my recommended advice to you at this time would be, at a minimum, to choose plan number one and decide to be a millionaire. Have you even heard anyone say, "Becoming a millionaire simply reduces to positioning yourself to become one," or "Being rich simply reduces to positioning yourself to be rich"? These were very precious words, like music to my ears a number of years ago, and served as one of my guiding lights to keep me going and enable me to stay committed. Perhaps these same words will be a guiding light for you as they were for me.

My hope will always be that each and every one of you shoot for and even have game plan number three within your sight and within your grasp, just as soon as it is possible. However, if game plan number three is not and never will be remotely possible, then, after you've made your biggest splash in investment properties and have become a "millionaire plus," my recommendation to you would be to follow game plan number two at that time and reduce your debt. As the old saying goes, "If you don't take control of it, it will take control of you." Debt is no different than anything else. However, going much further into debt can work great wonders, as I showed you in game plan number three, if you keep it manageable. Then, you'll be able to scavenge the real estate rewards, as I point out to you in chapter 12.

Key Point

- A desire to learn is key to success.
- Add and improve your skills to overcome liabilities.
- Jump right in at first, but plan a few steps ahead after. Getting your feet wet is a good idea, but planning and having a general idea of where you're going is necessary to succeed.
- You can bundle mortgages for lower interest rates.
- Find a mentor or mentors.
- Take calculated risks to maximize your earnings and expand your portfolio in the real estate riches game.

Six

Scavenging the
Deconstruction

Though not an everyday household word, the concept of *deconstruction* has been practiced by all societies since the beginning of mankind. In case you're unaware, it is a method of harvesting or reclaiming what is commonly considered "waste" and is sometimes referred to as "construction in reverse."

Deconstruction is commonly divided into two categories: structural and nonstructural, both of which I will comment about in great detail, through personalizing some of my own experiences.

Structural Deconstruction

Back in the mid-1950s, before my brother Bob and I knew anything about what was going on around us, our dad had purchased an old converted railroad car that we called home. Within days he began creating a board pile in our backyard (out of previously used lumber, of course) and started to talk about building a double garage. The next thing I remember, our dad gave Bob and I each our own hammer and showed us how to pull nails. Not only were we taught how to pull nails, but to separate the straight ones from the crooked ones so the better ones could be reused. Bob and I were five and four years old respectively. Since my dad became ill, due to acute asthma (as you will remember from earlier chapters), for most of the next eight years until he died, our only means of survival as a family was through the discards of others. These discards in one form or another came from deconstruction. Five years later, in 1960, though Bob and I were still only kids, our dad built a second double garage out of dismantled lumber from other buildings. This time, however, he declared us as his main "carpenter helpers," only employing a few men for a few hours here and there to do only what Bob and I couldn't do.

After my dad passed away, in my midteens, a controversy swirled in the air in my home village of Union, Iowa. Our local gravedigger and part-time farmer, Jake, was being ridiculed. One person sneered, "He surely doesn't know what he's doing." Another person added, "The house that old fool's building, all out of recycled lumber, will be the ugliest in town." Still another person declared, "I'll bet the wind will blow it over." In the 1960s the economy was booming, the lumber yards were recording record sales, and many considered it dumb or un-American to build using deconstructed materials.

Because of my background, I can't believe how "modern" our mind-set as a nation has become. Incidentally, old Jake's "new" house turned out as attractive as any of the other houses. A few years later, he told me on the street one day, "Steve, with the exception of buying new cedar siding, shingles, and a few other things, I used all recycled materials."

At this time I'd like to fast-forward a number of years. As I was getting back into real estate investing after about a 10-year hiatus, though I'd many times practiced nonstructural deconstruction (that of removing and transplanting kitchen cabinets, etc.), I hadn't really capitalized on structural deconstruction. Because I'd just purchased a 17-unit apartment building that needed much refurbishing, my conservative mind-set of seeking deconstructed materials was on a high state of alert. The local Medicap Pharmacy, which occupied an old filling station, had just moved to its new location only a few feet away, and their old building was about to be demolished.

As luck would have it, a neighbor mentioned that the old store was set to be knocked down the following Monday morning. At that very moment, my scavenger mind-set led me to the new store to talk to the owner, Ray. Instantly, and much to my surprise, he immediately said, "Steve, take all you want out of the old pharmacy building, but promise me you'll be long gone by Monday morning and that you won't interfere in any way with the demolition contractor." To make a long story short, the rolled fiberglass insulation alone, which I removed and transplanted into a large attic, was a huge windfall for me. I calculated it to be worth about $2,000, and that was in early 1990. It probably would be at least a $4,000 value in today's market. I not only got the insulation for free, but I was able to cut the fuel bill in half at the building where it was transplanted. My memory has faded as to the other items I removed, but to give you an idea, we removed two or three steel entry doors, a few windows, and interior wooden doors, among other items, including a water heater that I took to my office building—it is still working more than 20 years later.

Though it's more labor intensive to deconstruct, never underestimate the huge savings that await you, if you have a use for certain types of materials and a place to store them until you are ready to reuse them.

Nonstructural Deconstruction

Since becoming involved in real estate and the rental business, I have, by far, become more engaged in nonstructural deconstruction, as opposed to structural deconstruction. So, how can it be of benefit to you? Nonstructural deconstruction, also known as "self-stripping," consists of reclaiming nonstructural components. I personally think of it as all items that I can remove quickly from one property and transplant rather quickly at another. Note the list of examples that follow:

- Upper kitchen cabinets
- Lower kitchen cabinets
- Countertops, Formica, granite, Corian, etc.
- Kitchen sinks and faucets
- Kitchen breakfast bars and islands
- Refrigerators
- Stoves
- Dishwashers
- Microwaves
- Light fixtures (interior and exterior)
- Ceiling tile and grid
- Window trim, door trim, and baseboards
- Shelving
- Washers and dryers
- Vertical and horizontal blinds
- Curtains and drapes
- Thermostats
- Doors and some windows, locks, and handles
- Carpet
- Carpet pad
- Concrete and wooden steps and railings (easily removable)
- Switches, outlets, and covers
- Register and vent covers
- Furnaces, including baseboard heaters
- Central air conditioners
- Wall-mounted or window air conditioners
- Water heaters
- Humidifiers and dehumidifiers
- Electrical breaker panels or just the breakers
- Fireplace mantles
- Garage doors with electric openers
- Bathroom vanities and tops
- Bath tubs, hot tubs, and saunas
- Shower stalls
- Bath tub surrounds (certain types)

- Towel cabinets
- Toilets and toilet seats
- Mirrors
- Medicine cabinets
- Towel bars
- Closet poles and racks (wooden and metal)
- Ceiling fans
- Sump pumps
- Fencing (chain-link, vinyl, and wooden)
- Decks
- Lamp posts
- Pedestal-style and wall-mounted mailboxes

Many times I have benefited greatly by reutilizing these nonstructural items. At times I've been able to scavenge houses and apartment buildings and remove all I wanted for free. At other times I've had to pay a small but reasonable amount of money per house or per apartment unit before the building or buildings were demolished. Also, all of these materials are obtainable through other ways and means. As I've mentioned in previous chapters, don't forget various employees who have access to these things as well. Many of these people have a small business on the side, apart from their normal daytime job, and will sell deconstructed items to you at a very low cost. The following are examples of people in your neighborhoods to check with when your own stock runs low, thus avoiding having to buy something new at the last moment:

- Flooring installers (for carpet, pad, leftover vinyl pieces, etc.)
- Plumbers (for stools, vanities, showers, tubs, etc.)
- Electricians (for breaker panels, lamps, alarm systems, ceiling fans, etc.)
- Carpenters (for doors, windows, shelving, decking boards, countertops, etc.)
- Bricklayers (for reusable or discontinued bricks, step railings, etc.)
- Siding installers (for reusable siding, discounted siding, color varieties, etc.)

- Window and door installers (for specific types and odd measurements needed)
- Roofers (for color varieties and where to find sheeting, shingles, discounts, etc.)
- HVAC installers (for repaired, new, and used good-quality furnaces and ACs at low prices)
- Cabinet installers (for all kitchen-related items including good used cabinets at competitive prices)
- Appliance repairmen (for all types of used appliances at one-third or less their cost new)

So, how important is nonstructural deconstruction to the average real estate investor? Most of us in this business see it as essential to reduce rehab costs and at the same time increase the property's net worth and our own net worth in one of the shortest ways possible. Before we get to the end of this chapter, just to reiterate the importance of this topic, let me tell you about two guys in the deconstruction business, previous mentioned, who supply my Houston-area properties for all our needs. These two guys, Jay and Tee, are business partners. They've been in business quite a number of years and make their living as nonstructural deconstructors. Jay recently told me of obtaining a contract to non-structurally deconstruct a 600-unit apartment building 30 days before the cranes and bulldozers arrived to start demolition. I then said, "Jay, do you send in large groups of workers to dismantle everything?" He replied, "Oh, no, Steve, I just contact a bunch of landlords and property investors such as yourself, then I sell each of them the rights to scavenge or salvage large blocks of apartments, such as ten or twenty or more at a time, to remove all they want within a certain time frame." Jay went on, "If all the easy stuff isn't stripped away or if we don't get the salvage rights to all units sold before demolition day, Tee and I will go in with a group of men to remove what's left and take those things back to our yard."

Can you believe that, as I sat here writing, Jay called to let me know that he has secured the rights to non-structurally deconstruct yet another 600-unit apartment building? And, for whatever it's worth, they just recently took a 50-unit apartment building, to "give them something to do" while the paperwork gets done on the 600-unit complexes. Before I hung up the phone, I said, "Jay, have you ever deconstructed any larger structures bigger than six hundred units?" He said, "Oh, heck, yes, on a few occasions."

By the way, do any of you suppose it's at all possible to scavenge a scavenger? Well, that's precisely what I did with these guys. Not to take away from them or degrade them in anyway, because they're good people, but as you will see, there are times when even big-time scavengers need to cut a deal. A few weeks ago, I got a call from Tee. He said. "Steve, do you still need refrigerators?" I said, "Well, not really; I still have some in reserve from that last bunch you sold me." He then said, "Well, we need to move some product" (meaning, "Not much money has been coming in lately, and we're flat-ass broke at the moment."). He said, "Would you give one hundred and fifty dollars for some like new fridges, but less than the standard size?" I said, "Why would I when I bought the last batch for one hundred and twenty five dollars each?" Then, having forgotten what I'd paid the last time, Tee said, "Steve, today I'm ready to cut you one hell of a deal. If you can buy at least ten, you can have them for eighty dollars each." As the old saying goes, "When people are ready to deal, they're ready to deal!"

So, what's my message here in scavenging a scavenger? Always downplay the importance of any deal to the hilt in order to bring the other person to his or her lowest asking price. Though I didn't want Tee to know, we really did need those 10 additional refrigerators, and, of course, I never told him that he called me at a very opportune time!

As I end this chapter, I hope you understand the difference between structural and nonstructural deconstruction. In my opinion, "going green" by reducing as much waste as possible is very important to our environment, but also very important to the economic survival of entrepreneurs. Through deconstruction, we can gain a foothold in the very competitive business of refurbishing properties to rent or to sell and can scavenge our way to real estate riches.

Key Points

- Nonstructural deconstruction is always the quickest method to remove everything from a building without altering the structure itself. This includes the removal of items such as kitchen cabinets, appliances, carpet and pad, baseboards, windows and door trim, etc.
- Many contractors have building materials left over from jobs that can be purchased at considerable savings, as well as reserves of items, such as cabinets, countertops, and woodwork, removed from job sites before the new items are installed.
- Some building owners will allow scavengers to extract materials for free or at low cost simply to lower their tipping fees at the landfill.
- Before demolition, some building owners will contract out scavenging rights to scavengers looking for materials to salvage.
- One man's trash is another's treasure. Scavenged materials from one building can be worth upward of $5,000 to $10,000 for only a few dozen hours of work removing and transplanting certain materials.
- Never show desperation when negotiating for prices.
- When the time is right, it is possible for scavengers to scavenge from other scavengers on the road to real estate riches.

Seven

Scavenging
the Appreciation

This chapter will point out a variety of ways to create value in your properties. Whether you only have a single-family dwelling or hundreds of houses or apartments, these proven techniques will allow you to ask for and receive more money, especially if you're preparing your home for sale or expecting to charge more rent for a rental property.

Scavenged appreciation, otherwise known as forced appreciation, will usually allow you to recoup every dollar invested, enhance rentability or salability, and in many cases give you a huge return on your investment.

Interior

Space Utilization

Since I first got started in the rental business in the 1970s, I have been able to add great value to most of my properties, without adding square footage, by better utilizing the space I had. For example, at a single-family dwelling I bought only a few months ago (which incidentally is the subject and subtitle of my next book, *Shacks on* a *Shoestring*), I added great value to the property. By utilizing this technique of scavenging the appreciation, I figure I added at least several thousand dollars of value to this two-bedroom house by creating a third bedroom. We simply took the kitchen out of the room it was occupying and placed it at the end of the adjoining rectangular-shaped living room. By doing this, we immediately had a third bedroom of normal size without having added extra square footage to the house. Imagine how simple it is to use basic techniques such as this one. However, unless you begin to train yourself to think that way, you'll never be able to channel your thoughts in that direction when the time comes. Just think for a minute of the countless dozens of other would-be buyers who passed on this house, who couldn't see what I saw, not to mention all the other investors who couldn't see what I saw either! By adding a third bedroom in this way, this house experienced an immediate increase in value of at least $15,000. (See the following before and after diagrams.)

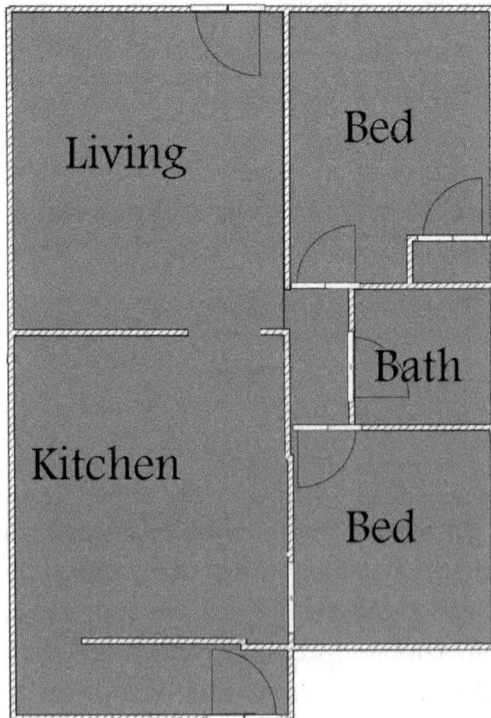

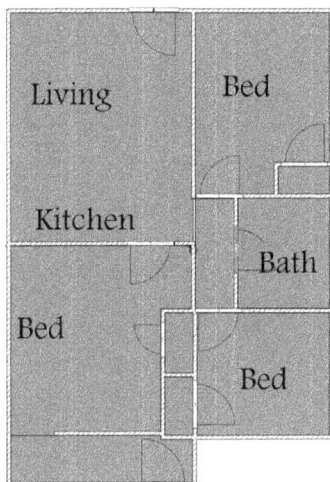

In a similar case a few years ago, I purchased another two-bed-room single-story house that had a very large three-season porch attached to the back side. As it was winter in Iowa, my first thoughts were to move a tenant into the house as quickly as possible, mainly to avoid paying the fuel bills while remodeling at the same time. As luck would have it, the tenant moved out during the summer the following year, freeing the house to be rehabbed, and allowing me to "scavenge" a great amount of appreciation and follow through with my plan at the time of purchase. Since the three-season porch had sidewalls, a nice cement floor, and a roof that didn't leak, and was very firmly attached to the rest of the house, I knew that for only a few thousand dollars investment, I could do wonders to the property. I hugely increased its overall value and current rent, work-ing with a scavenged laborer I found at the local halfway house, by dividing that large rectangular three-season porch in half, adding two additional bedrooms, thus converting the existing two-bedroom house into a four-bedroom house. The necessary costs of ceiling and sidewall insulation, four thermopane windows, a handful of 2x4s, sheetrock, two interior doors, carpet (see before and after diagrams that follow), and one scavenged laborer, combined with my own sweat equity, were miniscule compared to how much the property appreciated.

On the final day of rehab, before raising the monthly rent by $200, I spotted a realtor friend of mine showing a house for sale across the street. As he finished with his potential prospect, I said, "Hey, Bob, why don't you come over here and give me a quickie market analysis?" Within a few minutes, he said, "Steve, it surely ought to bring $57,900." Not too bad for only having paid $9,500 less than two years before!

Though I could write an entire book on scavenging the appreciation and probably a second book on utilization of space, let me end this segment by listing additional examples of how I utilized space to monetize rents to their maximum. This way you too may expand your horizons even further and increase the overall value of your properties and scavenge your way to profits in the real estate game.

- I converted an attached garage with a loft to a one-bedroom apartment.
- I converted a large one-bedroom apartment into two one-bedroom apartments by closing off a doorway, inserting a three-quarter bath into a closet, installing a new kitchen on the back wall of the existing kitchen so as to not have to run new plumbing, and converting a three-season porch into a bedroom, doubling the monthly rent in the process.
- I divided a large living room into two, which, though obviously reducing the size of the large living room, created a third bedroom.
- I removed washer and dryer hookups from unfinished basements and created main floor laundries, eliminating so many trips to the basement, enhancing value and rentability.
- I installed a second full bath in places, such as at the end of an extra-long bedroom, etc.
- I installed half-baths in closets, just large enough to do so, thus avoiding having to build a small room to house the half-bath.
- I converted a structure with three large apartments into a structure of eight apartments, consisting of studios and one-bedroom units.

You can employ scavenged or forced appreciation techniques to increase the value of your property, all without counting on inflation to do it for you or without waiting for your mortgage to pay down. Increasing value by improving the interior and exterior appearance of the property is essential.

Improving the General Décor

Of course, your budget will determine how extensive you can be in improving the general décor, without going beyond the point of diminishing returns. What do I mean by that? Well, to use a ridiculous example, you wouldn't want to infuse $15,000 in constructing or reconstructing a fireplace (regardless of how stunningly precious it may be guaranteed to look when finished) if the maximum value of the small, one-bedroom house in question in a bad area of town would only be $40,000.

To begin, one of the easiest things you can do that costs very little and that is always quite effective is simply to paint all the rooms and, in some cases, paint all the woodwork, too. The second easiest thing to do is to clean. As most of you already know, these two things, painting and cleaning, give us the "biggest bang for our buck," as we sometimes say. Beyond that, some of the other simple, less costly measures we can take are as follows:

- Install crown molding, particularly in the main entry room.
- Change all baseboards, window trim, and door trim to an attractive type of wood, such as light, medium, or dark oak, or at least paint what's there with a contrasting color.
- If your budget will allow it, change all interior doors to match the new window trim, door trim, and baseboards, or paint all of them the same contrasting color used on the rest of the woodwork.
- Window treatments, such as vertical or horizontal blinds, curtains, drapes, etc., go a long way in improving appearance as well.

- Ceiling fans with the blades painted or stained and varnished to match the rest of the woodwork also pay dividends.
- Changing all the rounded door knobs or handles to lever-type handles throughout the house is a small amount of money well spent.
- Register and air vent covers should be changed or at least painted.
- New or very clean electrical outlet covers and switch plate covers that are all the same color is also a small but important improvement.

Kitchens

Apart from adding a breakfast bar or an island to the kitchen (which at this time is very popular), your biggest concern should be the appearance of the upper and lower cabinets. Once again, install all new cabinets if your budget allows. If not, there are many companies that can make them look brand new by simply refacing them for an economical price. And, of course, if the house is an old fixer-upper that you bought cheap but want to dump in a hurry, you'll only want to prime them, then paint them with a good-quality enamel. While you're at it, you'll want to either resurface the countertop or change it to a new one. Then don't forget to stick in a nice new sink, so shiny and nice, without any bumps or scratches, of course. Last, but not least, modern-looking appliances are a must if you can't afford new ones. As I did contract painting for a number of years, it was very easy for me to paint refrigerators here and there, eliminating nicks, scuffs, and scratches and making them look brand new. I would suggest, though, that if you can't paint the whole appliance or at least remove a blemish, rendering it unnoticeable, with a can of spray enamel, then change the appliance for one without blemishes or buy a new one. Another consideration is to remove the stove and refrigerator, leaving only the dishwasher and perhaps the built-in microwave in place. Let's face it, some kitchens show just as well, or even better, if some or all appliances are removed.

Baths

As we know, many things can be done to create added value in bathrooms. Here, again, the trick is to spend the least amount of money but have the greatest impact. The inexpensive costs of a new tub, fiberglass surround, and new faucets are worthwhile; these three things alone will be most eye catching. Beyond that, replacing the vanity and putting down a new vinyl floor run close behind in second place. However, in the last three or four bathrooms I've rehabbed, I've produced startling effects by installing an oak toilet seat, oak towel racks, oak towel cabinets, an oak toilet paper holder, an oak medicine cabinet, an oak light fixture (running across the top of the medicine cabinet with six bulbs), an oak vanity, and oak handles on the vanity sink faucet. Also, don't forget to install a new set of sliding glass doors on the tub, or, if your budget is meager, the least you should do is hang a very attractive shower curtain, with a new pole and set of hooks. There's one last thing I'd like to include that may help some of you. On a few occasions, I've bought large mirrors and installed them in small bathrooms, on one wall, and sometimes on two walls, making the room appear much bigger and more attractive to potential buyers.

Flooring

Except for improving the energy efficiency of the property, and staging the property, which we'll get to shortly, the last big category is flooring. Unless the property you're preparing to sell or rent has excellent flooring with perfect color patterns, you'll need to make some changes. If you're preparing a house to sell, whether it's one you've been renting or one you've recently purchased for resale, because of off colors, wear patterns, and so on, don't count on being able to salvage more than one or two out of five rooms of flooring material. Your first option should be to try to strip down and refinish all rooms of hardwood flooring that you discover. This procedure doesn't take that long, and, even if you don't have that particular type of sander at your disposal, paying to rent one is not that expensive.

If that option isn't available to you, then you need to consider one or more of the following different types of flooring: VCT (vinyl composition tile), ceramic tile, carpet, vinyl, laminate, or hardwood. Unless you're preparing to sell an old fixer-upper, or what is sometimes called a handyman special, except for utilizing transplantable scavenged carpet, the rest of these materials can't be found as secondhand materials and, of course, will have to be purchased new. That's not to say you can't find factory closeouts and discontinued brands of new flooring materials that have been greatly discounted, because you can. Just be patient and start stocking up a few weeks or months ahead of time, and you'll be on the positive side of the ledger. As the topic of stocking up crops up at this time, let's all be reminded that one of the big keys to successfully investing and having available scavenged or discounted materials when you need them without being at the mercy of retailers at the last minute is also having a storage place to contain and organize your stockpiles!

Energy Efficiency

Another way to ensure that your property experiences an increase in value is to be able to show that it's energy efficient and that the tenant or new owner can heat and cool the structure for a less than average amount of money. You also could get a printout of recent heating and cooling costs from the local utility company, comparing your home to that of other houses of the same square footage, to show that yours is considerably less costly to heat and cool. Any prospective tenant or new owner would make note of that and immediately begin to think that the house is of greater value. Except for a few minor exceptions, such as filling foundation cracks or installing low E windows that absorb more heat in the winter and reflect more heat in the summer, the only other way to obtain the greatest amount of energy efficiency is by updating your heating and cooling system and insulation levels. For one thing, you must have adequate sidewall, ceiling, and, in some cases, roof insulation. It's never cost-effective to make the sidewalls thicker, but it is sometimes cost-effective to apply a type of insulation board to the outer walls of the house before deciding to attach a more modern kind of siding, both of which boost value. In this day and age, it would be very rare in America to find a house without some ceiling insulation. However, a huge number of houses currently have a very inadequate amount of ceiling insulation. This ends up costing tenants and homeowners a bundle. "It is like money thrown to the wind," as my mother used to say. Therefore, at a minimum, check the level of insulation in your attic. For whatever it's worth, our utility provider in Iowa told us a few years ago that we needed about 10 to 12 inches of insulation in our attics before reaching the point of diminishing returns. Fast-forward to today, and that same utility company tells its customers they need 16 inches in their attics. Unless you're 100% sure of what the attic insulation level should be in your area, you most probably would be money ahead to put this book down at this moment; grab a ladder, a tape measure, and a flash light; and personally measure the attic insulation in your home.

Lastly, since almost our entire population has some form of heating and/or cooling source in their homes, making sure your furnace and central air conditioner, or window or wall units, are of high efficiency is of great importance. Let's look at this from a different angle. If you have your home in relatively good condition but have an obsolete heating and cooling system, do you suppose a prospective tenant or potential buyer might pass on the deal because of that? The answer is that they might! Who wants to pay an extra $100 or so per month that's unnecessary? Unless there was something exceptionally unique about the property, only a fool would be interested. What's more, most new buyers don't have several extra thousand dollars lying around to be able to modernize the heating and cooling system, even if they wanted to, after completing the purchase. So, to enhance rentability or salability, be prudent and update your furnace and air conditioners as you scavenge your way to real estate success.

Staging

Curb appeal, or visual appeal, is an important part of renting or selling, but few renters or buyers really make up their minds until they've seen the property on the inside. Only then is the importance of staging realized. Staging is really nothing more than putting furniture in a home to simulate an active living space and to help a prospective renter or owner get an idea of what it might be like to live there. This technique not only speeds up the renting or selling process, but also is known to artificially force value upward, or "scavenge" additional value out of thin air. Conservative estimates show that staged houses yield 6% more money than unstaged homes. (This number can go as much as 17% higher.) Also, not figured into this is the time a home might remain on the market and how many $900 to $1,200 monthly mortgage payments you might be making while the home sits empty. This is also not to mention heating and cooling costs, taxes, insurance, and so forth. Considering this scenario, spending $2,000 to $3,000 for a professional home staging company doesn't seem like such a bad idea. Since many of you are buying more modest houses in the $35,000 to $100,000 range, my suggestion is still to stage the property but to use an alternative method. Since $2,000 to $3,000 is a lot of money for some of you, for only a few hundred dollars, you could pick up just enough good-looking furniture at an estate sale or have friends or family loan you a few pieces if your budget is nonexistent. In the Des Moines, Iowa, metro area, with a population of about 630,000, for example, there are 10 companies with websites that do staging. Looking at other listings, there are almost 50 smaller businesses and independent contractors and consultants doing this work.

In a recent phone conversation with my sister in Amarillo, Texas, the topic of staging came up. She said, "Oh, Steve, what a huge difference that made for us when we sold out last house." She went on, "After an eternity had passed, we changed to realtors who staged the house for us, and in lightning speed it sold for more than we thought we'd ever get."

Exterior

Now that we've covered scavenging the appreciation as it applies to the interior to boost the value of a property, let's turn to the exterior.

As difficult as it is to divide up and classify the different facets of scavenging exterior appreciation, I have broken it into four separate categories: landscaping, aesthetics, additions, and miscellaneous.

Landscaping

For this section, I define landscaping as arranging or modifying features of the land for practical reasons. Though I probably won't include every last detail, the major components will be included. To begin, to make your property more valuable, rid the ground of all debris, trim all trees and bushes, remove any and all dead limbs, and cut the grass. Of course, leveling the ground wherever necessary, sowing grass seed, and at times laying down sod in strategic areas is also a must.

Turning to electrical considerations, don't be afraid to install ground lights along the edge of the sidewalk, driveway, or both, and don't overlook a lamp pole and possibly a yard light mounted to the front or side of the house. And, don't forget the idea of going solar. I recently installed exterior solar lights, which in most cases are cost effective to install from a labor and materials standpoint and decrease electric bills.

Before we move on to aesthetics, don't forget the importance of a driveway in good condition. If it's made of asphalt, you can fill the cracks and seal coat it for only pennies per square foot. If it consists of only dirt and grass, a load of gravel also goes a very long way to improve the look of the property. Concrete will always cost you more, but sometimes it is the only option, and, on the plus side, people always associate concrete with value, especially new concrete.

While we're on the topic of concrete, don't overlook the condition of your sidewalk. Even if many sections are cracked and are in need of replacement, every penny will be well spent.

Aesthetics

Aesthetics is often defined as a sense of beauty, appreciating beautiful things, or having to do with the qualities of beauty. Doing something as simple as painting to beautify a property can force upward, or scavenge, the appreciation of your property. Though everything hinges on the strength of your budget, painting earns the best value for the money. And, not only painting, but strategically painting your property brings in even greater rewards. For example, assuming that the house is completely paintable—that is not consisting of vinyl or brick siding, etc.—you would never elect to paint it all one color. Why? Because two colors are always more attractive than one! Therefore, to maximize the effect, you most likely would choose two colors, one as a base color and a second color to paint the trim. A good suggestion to follow in painting trim would be to not only paint around the doors and windows, but to also include the fascia board, the vertical corner boards (if any), and the foundation if possible, even if it's only slightly noticeable. While you're at it, don't hesitate to stretch your imagination and paint the mailbox with that same trim paint, the enclosure for the trash cans or for your trash bin if you have a rental property, and so on, and so forth.

Before leaving the topic of low-cost aesthetics, don't forget the importance of shutters. Of course, they have no practical value, but if you really want to dress up a property for not much money and they aren't already attached, shutters are the way to go, even if your local home improvement store doesn't have your color and painting is required before mounting them.

Moving on to other aesthetics, covering the fascia and soffeting with white or colored aluminum instead of just painting, not to mention through a new layer of shingles or by hanging vinyl siding, you can reap big dividends as well. Then you could even consider (if it's cost-effective) employing a bricklayer to do a bit of brick or brick veneer work to the front of the property. Though brickwork usually isn't recommended because of the cost, in some cases it can be cost-effective. As an old bricklayer friend, Bruno, from East Prussia, used to say, "There ain't nothing too expensive if you can afford it, and for you, Steve, I give special price." Because the word *quality* is so strongly associated with brickwork, I'd highly recommend you do one or two things with bricks, such as build a base for your mailbox if it stands alone, create a birdbath or planter box for flowers, amplify the base of a flag pole, and so forth.

Before moving on to my next category, I want to touch on windows and doors, as well as gutters and downspouts. It has been my experience that when employing these techniques to enhance rentability or salability, obsolete-looking windows and doors stand out like sore thumbs and need to be changed to make the property appear more modern, not to mention their R-factor, making the residence more energy efficient. Lastly, since gutters and downspouts come in a variety of colors, have their color match your trim paint color upon installation, as I've done many times. Not only will they add value because they are practical, but also because they definitely beautify your property. Also, don't forget to remind yourself that gutters and downspouts can be painted to find that perfect contrast you need if the existing ones are in good shape and don't need to be replaced.

Additions

Other things you can do to the exterior of a property that quickly boost its value, that give you a return on your money, and that stunningly attract the attention of the would-be buyer or tenant are as follows: repair, beautify, assemble, or build from scratch a carport, a storage shed, a deck, a sun porch, or an open or closed patio, and, while you're at it, don't rule out the great return on your money that fencing can bring. Before commenting individually about these things, let me briefly mention the possibility of adding a garage. I will discuss garages separately because almost never, except in rare circumstances, can you gain a return on your investment by building a garage, though you definitely can increase the value and attractiveness. This alone may be just enough to rent or sell an otherwise difficult property. If that is true, then losing a few dollars to build a garage from scratch might be the best way to turn an "easy profit."

Now I will comment briefly on the other six topics included under additions that, if assembled or constructed properly with an emphasis on holding down spending, will make you money. At the very least, if you only barely break even on the cost of labor and materials, if they have greatly enhanced your ability to rent or sell quickly, in every case it will have been worth it. In the case of a carport, even if you are in a hurry and skip using scavenged labor and materials, you will add far more value to the property than the overall costs to construct it. In recent years, Americans have put far more emphasis on the topic of storage than ever before. Though my first suggestion would be to build a storage shed out of scavenged labor and materials, if you're patient and watch the ads in your local newspaper or on Craigslist, great bargains are waiting to be found, and even though you'll have to disassemble, transport, and then reassemble the one you find in an ad, the cost to purchase a secondhand one should be miniscule. Even brand-new models at home improvement centers are very economically priced if the temptation to buy a new one is too great. As far as adding a sun porch, this can be done very economically, but only if you have one of those houses designed in such a way that begs of you to build it. Yes, there really are houses that are very ripe for sun porch additions. Of course, if you don't have this type of situation crying out to you, spend your improvement dollars on other things.

Decks and patios, on the other hand, can add aesthetic value to a property and are usually easy and fairly economical to construct. Once again, some residences, because of their design, beg you each time you walk through to "put a deck here" or "build a patio in this spot." Even updating an existing deck or patio can do wonders. Last year I had the urge to replace the railings and floor boards of the deck at my house, and I headed to the nearest Habitat for Humanity ReStore. As I had in mind to buy composite boards—almost prohibitively too expensive, but they never fade or peel—I arrived and went through the main entrance. After explaining to the clerk what I wanted, she said, "Sorry, someone came in yesterday and bought a whole truck load, reducing our stock to nothing. It was a manufacturer's closeout and we had so much, we let it go very cheap." I'm still kicking myself for having missed such a good deal. However, let this be a lesson to you that expensive materials do exist at greatly reduced prices, if you know where to look and are vigilant at scavenging bargains.

Fencing, which I could have included under landscaping or aesthetics, be it chain-link, wood, or vinyl, if strategically placed, can increase the value of your property, can be cost-effective, and can make it dynamically appealing. For practical use, privacy, or for aesthetics, just a small amount of fencing placed here or there will sometimes put your property in a category all by itself, drawing unprecedented attention, quickly finding a new tenant or buyer and adding to your real estate–generated wealth.

Miscellaneous

Lastly, don't overlook the little odds and ends that can have an impact. For example, wouldn't we all agree that house numbers are important? Just think back to the times you've tried to locate a particular house and were unable to because of the absence or lack of visibility of the numbers. How about installing a shiny brass kickplate to the bottom of the entrance door to match a new shiny brass bolt lock. While you're at it, why not change the older rounded door knob to a new shiny brass lever-handled one? Couldn't you even carry this simple idea a little further and change your wall-hung mailbox to a shiny brass one, and how about the door bell, the lamp above the door, and so on? The little things at times can be huge and should be considered, especially when the time and the costs involved are so small.

Key Points

- Investigate ways to reutilize space to create extra rooms, such as an additional bedroom, a laundry room, closets, etc.
- Enhance the curb appeal of your home by replacing inexpensive items including doorknobs, vent covers, outlet covers, mailboxes, driveway lights, fencing, etc.
- Use contrasting colors to improve visual appeal on the exterior of the building.
- Improve the appearance of kitchens and bathrooms to make the house more appealing.
- Replace damaged flooring, and try to utilize previously scavenged materials to keep costs down.
- Improve energy efficiency with more modern heating and cooling, double-pane windows, and better insulation.
- Improve overall curb appeal by landscaping the front lawn and staging the interior, which will make the home more likely to sell quickly or rent for more money.
- Improve the value of the property with additions such as decks, carports, patios, a fence, etc.

Eight

Scavenging
the Expertise

Have you ever heard the expression, "The bigger your network, the bigger your net worth"? Since I personally have found these words to be true, my suggestion to you, especially if you're looking to prosper and to grow your business, is to repeat those words a few times each day until they become fully implanted in your thoughts.

As you expand your business, you'll immediately begin to see that assembling your team and growing your network will be crucial if you are to succeed. As a result, your network will consist of specialists, each in different individualized fields, each with separate knowledge to share with you, to help your business run more smoothly, and to propel you through each and every goal, all in the shortest length of time.

So, just who are these mini-mentors, specialists, and people of knowledge who will be so crucial to your success? I will first list many, if not most, of the titles of these specialists who will eventually find their way into your network and who will contribute greatly to the build-up of your net worth as you seek to scavenge your way to real estate riches.

Categories of scavengable expertise:

- Attorneys
- Realtors
- CPAs
- Bookkeepers/accountants
- Title companies
- Sheriffs or deputies
- Policemen
- Bank loan/default officers
- Finance company managers
- Business partners
- Other landlords
- Other investors
- City inspectors
- City assessors
- Appraisers
- Real Estate Birddogs
- Computer operators/specialists
- Structural engineers
- Financial planners
- Courthouse employees
- City hall employees
- Surveillance companies
- Auctioneers
- Pest controllers
- Stagers
- Deconstructors
- General contractors
- Rehab contractors
- Subcontractors
- Pawn shop owners
- Sign shop owners
- Secondhand store owners
- Habitat for Humanity employees

- Home improvement store department managers
- REIA members
- Mentors

As I look back on my 37 years of real estate investing, it instantly becomes so clear how much my team of experts helped me reach my financial goals. In other words, only a fool would think that he or she could really go it alone and still achieve great success.

Not only do you not want to go it alone, but as you select your team members, decide upon the most knowledgeable at the least amount of cost, something I commonly refer to as scavengable expertise, which should be your number one goal.

Attorneys

In searching for legal help, for example, especially if you're dead broke, an obvious team member you'll need from the very start, upon making your first real estate purchase, will be an attorney. Therefore, why not choose one who has retired, who wants to give back to the community? They are virtually everywhere and easy to locate. They usually will give you a certain amount of their time and will show you how to find the proper forms on the Internet, if not even make a court appearance with you, all for free.

A second option might be to find an attorney involved in real estate investing who would be willing to barter, to allow you to trade your maintenance skills for a few hours of legal work.

If you're really rock bottom low on funds, as all of us investors are at different times in our investing careers, why not distinguish your résumé with a few testimonials from people you've done a variety of work for and present it to a real estate investor attorney? If you're good at property managing, maintenance, or both, and do a good job at selling yourself, you will definitely find an attorney willing to barter!

Having said that, you still can scavenge the best situation for yourself, even by going the conventional route in selecting an attorney, if you simply take time to use your head. What do I mean by that? Well, assuming that most will charge you a minimum of at least $150 per hour, regardless of what type of work you need to have done, why not choose an attorney who specializes in real estate? Not only that, but why stop there? Why not choose an attorney who dedicates some of his or her time to the type of real estate investing in which you are involved? Now, let's expand this example a little further. Why not search for and find an attorney who not only has some knowledge of real estate, not only of the type you're involved in, but who also is an investor in real estate and, at the same time, is dedicated to the same kind of real estate investments as yourself?

Besides, when the time comes, you'll have plenty of time to make those two or three extra phone calls, to filter through those in your area, to find the right attorney for you. Utilizing an attorney who invests, or has invested exactly the way you do, will pay huge dividends and will be a much easier individual with whom to communicate. Imagine what it will feel like to always be able to speak the same language, and to always be on the same page, as the attorney you have selected, who always knows where you're coming from with all your questions? Besides, he or she will usually only charge you the same rate as other competitors. Also, if you have good chemistry, he or she will more than likely find a good purchase or two for you every now and then and even perhaps invite you to partner on a few deals. And, if that happens, at that point, you will surely get most of your legal work done for only a nominal fee, if not for free!

Realtors

From only dabbling in real estate to making it a full-time career, you will have to deal with realtors at some point in time. Just like attorneys and other members of your team of expertise, their services can be scavenged.

As with selecting an attorney, find a realtor with whom you're on the same page. For example, he or she may be experienced, but overwhelmingly prefers to sell only single-family homes valued at a quarter of a million dollars or higher. He or she might be a great person, even someone with whom you have terrific chemistry, but don't be fooled! This realtor may convince you that he or she can indeed help you in every way but will be completely out of his or her element.

Just keep filtering through your list until you find a realtor who is genuinely sympathetic to your needs, someone who doesn't mind dabbling with the fixer-uppers. Though their commissions will be considerably less than selling "normal houses," simply convince them that they can have 100% of all your business. And, if the realtor works hard for you, promise that no other realtor in the area will sell you a house except through them. Lastly, sweeten the pot even further by offering them the resale of the same houses they just sold you—after they are rehabbed, of course.

However, a realtor who can find you great buys on all the fixer-uppers takes you only halfway there. That's right! The real realtor you're searching for needs to understand creative financing.

Just as with attorney's skills, use the same process to sum up the skills of a realtor. If he or she is not receptive to your needs, keep looking.

Once you've found a realtor who will help you find and "creatively finance" your deals, you are almost there, but you still will be a couple steps short of having found your "perfect realtor."

So, what's left? Where do you go from here? You'll know you've found the "perfect realtor" only if seller financing is not available on your current deal and your realtor decides to personally finance it. At this point, you simply find out if the realtor would be willing to contribute his or her commission to make the deal work, becoming your temporary or permanent partner until the property is sold, refinanced, or reappraised, whereby you would pull out equity, or until you can repay the commission used by your realtor as the down payment over several months or years.

If you get this far, you'll be 90% successful. To completely solidify your relationship, you simply need to convince this realtor that if he or she contributes all his or her commission toward the down payment, you would be the greatest business partner ever. And that because of your maintenance and management skills, all would run smoothly. Simply convince this realtor, at least on some deals, that within six months to a year, the property could be resold at a huge profit for both of you, splitting the increase in value 50-50 after 100% of the down payment money, plus interest, is returned to him.

In other words, show the realtor that you're so strong in property maintenance and management that he would never have to lift a finger except to sign the purchase contract beside your name upon obtaining the fixer-upper and sign again beside your name upon selling the same fixer-upper a few months to a year or two down the road.

As you finish this initial conversation with the realtor, a few additional references to the "mini pot of gold" that soon awaits both of you should be just enough to get his attention to tip the balance in your favor, to finally have your newly found realtor and business partner utter the little three-letter affirmation, *yes*, that drives all of us in so many ways.

Before ending this segment on realtors, to get him or her to bite on your proposal, you can also promise to throw into the deal, say, an extra thousand dollars or two, if he uses all of his commission to finance the deal, in the form of a promissory note, to be paid in full upon the sale of the property, or in monthly payments plus a reasonable rate of interest, for a specified period of time.

Now, let me tell you about an experience that happened to me just a few years ago. After deciding to purchase more multifamily housing in one of a few key cities in the great state of Texas, I made a call to my old friend and commercial real estate agent, Harry. The conversation went something like this: "Hey there, Harry, this is Steve Ames. How's the world treating you?" After a bit of chitchat, then explaining what I had in mind to purchase, Harry replied, "Steve, if you can hang on for another week or two, there's a one-hundred-and-fifty-unit complex about to go into bankruptcy that has your name written all over it!"

To make a long story short, Harry wanted to be my 50-50 partner in the deal. From the beginning he was willing to contribute 100% of his commission—3% of 2.5 million dollars, or $75,000. However, because of a bit of financial entanglement on a deal gone bad in a different partnership, Harry's credit score had dropped below an acceptable level, and he couldn't qualify to be 50% owner on the new loan.

Nonetheless, I've included this personal experience to show you just how easy it might be for you, too, to get a realtor to be a possible business partner as you work toward real estate success through honing your scavenging expertise.

Secondhand Store Owners and Managers

Though Habitat for Humanity is the name of a chain of secondhand stores found in 49 of the 50 states in the United States, employing plenty of workers and store managers who will let you scavenge their expertise, don't overlook owners and managers of the small secondhand stores. They can be a tremendous resource in passing along information to you pertaining to what they already have in stock, when they expect shipment or delivery of something specific that you urgently need, or for whatever items that came in unexpectedly that they for sure will set aside, just for you. Taking the time to get to know these employees and store owners, and by creating a special rapport with them, can save you time and money in many ways. Just in a simple phone conversation without having to make a special trip to see for yourself, they can give you many valuable details.

For example, if it's a secondhand furnace in question, they can tell you the age, the brand, the number of BTUs, the condition, the color, the height and width, their best price, and whether or not it includes delivery.

In the early 1990s, I myself was one of those secondhand store owners for a three-year period. Though I sold the business at a very profitable time, I continue to wonder how much more profitable Steve's Used Furniture would have been if only the name of my business had been Steve's Preowned Resale Center? This is a neat bit of information...just in case you too are contemplating starting your own store?

In any event, I made my business more successful by keeping phone numbers and name lists and maintaining good contact with customers looking for certain items, as well as with other business owners and landlords in need of specifics, such as coin-op washers and dryers, refrigerators, electric and gas stoves, air conditioners, furnaces, certain measurements or styles of doors and windows, and so forth.

Before closing this section on secondhand store owners and managers, let me make brief reference to a little store that just recently seemed to spring up out of the blue in my hometown. From what I understand, the store is open only three days each week and is run by volunteer labor from various churches, with all the store's contents donated by people in the community. In this store, you not only see lots of miscellaneous merchandise, but loads of building materials— a gold mine for any investor doing rehabbing.

Upon entering this store for the first time, I couldn't believe my eyes and began to ask questions. I discovered that the store's originator gets large construction companies to donate all their leftover materials from building and remodel projects, then donates all the proceeds to one or more countries in east Africa.

In any event, what a "gold mine find" this little store was for me, as I've just finished transforming a little "bulldoze-able shack" into a little "mini palace." So, just keep your eyes and ears open, as they say, and some good things may come your way, as they did for me.

Department Managers and Assistants

Department managers and their assistants can be an excellent source of knowledge, as well, particularly at home improvement stores like Lowe's, Menards, Home Depot, and so on. These store employees are usually eager to assist you, as a function of their employment, and can share some very important money-saving tips.

In case you are unaware, at all Menards stores throughout the United States that handle appliances, they make available to the public a large variety of used appliances, as well as new ones. The used ones are those given to the delivery drivers by the customers and brought back to the store to be sold as used merchandise. As you might imagine, these used appliances consist of gas and electric stoves, water heaters, refrigerators and freezers, microwaves, air conditioners, and so on. These used appliances are made available to the public for only $19 each but are guaranteed for two weeks. In other words, if the used appliance conks out within the first 14 days, you can return it for a full refund of $19, no questions asked.

By this time you must be asking yourself how to scavenge the expertise. You start by simply networking with the manager or assistant manager in the appliance department. Within a short time, you should be able to learn when the next appliance delivery is or when the delivery truck is set to return, if a delivery is in process at that moment.

Your next step will be to make personal contact with those employed or contracted by Menards to make the deliveries. Then, once you discover you have at least some degree of chemistry with at least one or more of the delivery drivers, you'll be almost there.

At that point simply say, "Hey, I'm in need of good used appliances for my rental properties." You may continue by saying, "For every good-looking stove, refrigerator, etc., you handle that I'm able to obtain, I'll gladly give you a cash bonus of fifty dollars." In my opinion, though $50 doesn't buy much these days, I'm quite certain those delivery drivers will have your cell phone number memorized in a heartbeat. Even if you found yourself handling far more used appliances than you could use for your own needs, nothing will be lost. You still can resell them to the public or to other landlords for a nifty little profit, making it well worth your time.

Just as a side note, for whatever it's worth, developing this kind of wheeler-dealer spirit will be important if you are to really succeed in the real estate business. At this moment if you find yourself saying, "But I never could see myself creating a special rapport with delivery drivers or offering an incentive for them to call me," you might need to reexamine your approach to business if you really want to be successful.

Before leaving this topic of department managers and assistants, all of the large home improvement stores seem to have what are known as bargain bins. Buying from these bargain bins is an excellent way to find good-quality products at greatly reduced prices. Though you will be buying products that have been discontinued or returned items that have been scuffed, scratched, or gouged, you'll be instantly money ahead. Furthermore, you may come across products that are closeout items. At other times you may find a bargain bin, for instance, full of brand-new, unscuffed, but mis-measured windows. When I was fast and furiously remodeling old fixer-uppers, as I still sometimes do, most of the time the window opening had to be slightly altered anyway, and a custom-grade window that measures a half inch longer or wider than a standard measurement makes not a single bit of difference yet is purchasable oftentimes for 50 cents on the dollar or less.

So when does scavenging the expertise come into play? The same way as I just described in reference to appliance department managers. Simply make personal contact with managers or their assistants in one or more of the departments, such as in building materials, floor coverings, millwork, and so forth. Then offer to do them some kind of favor in exchange for their information.

Of course, the kind of information you need from them will be in the form of answers to questions, such as when certain brands of windows, doors, and so forth will be classified as "discontinued" or slashed to 50% of the original asking price, and so forth. Also, the types of questions you'll need to have answers for will be questions like this: "Do you currently have in your bargain bin a solid or hollow-core door in a frame that measures thirty-six by eighty inches?" Another question might be something like, "Do you currently have any type of flooring material in your bargain bin, such as ceramic tile, VCT tile, or vinyl?"

Though offering cash as a tip for their information might be inappropriate, offering to do them a favor during their off-hours definitely would not be. Also, finding out what they like to talk about will be a big help to you. Who knows, you might discover you have a ton of things in common and become the best of friends. Then think for a minute how often your cell phone would ring, just at the most opportune time?

Real Estate Investors Association Members

Another indispensable part of your team, that's always available at a "scavengable rate," is the mentoring you receive from other REIA members, once you join a Real Estate Investors Association. In case you are unaware, REIA is an organization found in most large cities throughout the United States. A random sampling of the

Internet, for example, shows that there are 40 REIAs in California, 9 in Colorado, 22 in Texas, 8 in Wisconsin, 14 in Ohio, 40 in Florida, and so forth. You pay only a pittance to become a member—$120 per year, to be exact, at Two Rivers REIA of Central Iowa, where I'm a member. However, being mentored by other real estate investors from a variety of backgrounds is hugely invaluable to you.

REIA members consist of people from a wide range of occupations and professions. The free sharing of information by so many like-minded people is such a great asset to have at your disposal virtually anytime you decide to reach for the phone. Or you can attend one of the one or two monthly meetings.

The Two Rivers REIA here in Central Iowa, for example, has over 70 members. I jokingly tell people, because of the diverse backgrounds of our members, that our group consists of "butchers, bakers, candlestick makers, doctors, lawyers, and Indian chiefs." Really, though, to give you a true idea, the following is an actual abbreviated list of some of our current and past members' occupations or job titles:

- Doctors
- Lawyers
- Dentists
- Realtors
- Bankers
- Electricians
- Plumbers
- HVAC technicians
- Past builders
- Present builders
- Retired military
- Business executives
- Property managers
- Rehabbers
- Contractors

- Financial planners
- Computer systems engineers
- Software engineers
- Information technology people
- Insurance agents
- Sales professionals
- Accountants
- Water works engineers
- Full-time investors
- Firemen
- Teachers

In my opinion, anytime you can speed up the process, you gain knowledge in a particular area and get a job done more economically with much less hassle. This is why joining a REIA is so worthwhile for beginning and even seasoned investors. At the REIA where I belong, we always set aside time at each meeting for everyone to ask questions and share information. This is what we call our time for haves and wants. Some members will stand and tell about a property or properties they have for sale, others will talk about wanting to buy a particular style of house or perhaps a multifamily complex, yet a third person might share his or her need to find a special skills person to help complete a certain task.

Several months ago I was at a REIA meeting when one of our members stood up and spoke about waterproofing a basement. After collecting several bids, he finally found a small company, far more economical than the rest, that specialized in waterproofing and foundation wall repairs. The REIA member shared with us that this particular contractor did the work for 50% less than the lowest of all other bidders and that his work quality was superior.

A few weeks ago the subject of pest control came up. After a fairly lengthy discussion as to which pest control companies in the area charged the least for the services rendered, one of our members stood up and asked, "Why pay out all that money?" He went on to say, "Why not order all your chemicals for bedbugs, roaches, etc. the way I do at www.doityourselfpestcontrol.com, do the work yourself or hire it done in house, and save tons of money in the process?"

Just two nights ago, at our last REIA meeting, the subject of pest control came up again. One fellow member said, "In case you have to be certified in your community to handle the more potent chemicals, why not get the 7-A certification?" He continued, "I simply bought the exam booklet for thirty-five dollars, then paid twenty-five to take the test, and became certified."

As this chapter ends, I hope you have been reminded that there is almost always a more efficient and economical way to get things done. I only wish I could have said more about all the areas of expertise I listed.

Key Points

- Network with people who have common interests.
- Share your knowledge and help.
- Find like-minded people as friends and colleagues.
- Go out of your way to be a friend to someone and help him or her when needed.
- Educate yourself in some way, particularly in your area of business.
- Seek out the expertise and advice of others.
- Read as much as you can about your field.
- Follow the changing trends of your industry.
- Attend workshops and coaching sessions.
- Go to boot camps and seminars.
- Have a mentor, and be a mentor to someone else.
- Expand the ways you can scavenge your way to real estate riches.

Nine

Scavenging
the Fixed Costs

Many years ago, after having been in the rental business seemingly forever, I began to hear people talk about energy savings. After all, gasoline, for example, was cheap, and not much was said about gas mileage. Likewise, natural gas and electricity were also cheap, and not much attention was paid to the word *efficiency*. However, as time passed and as energy prices began to rise significantly, far more emphasis was placed on household appliances that would save you money.

Then one day, a friend in the rental business said to me, "Steve, don't you realize some of those big old refrigerators are costing you a lot of money?" I was completely caught off guard and responded, "What on earth are you talking about?" After all, they seemed to run forever without breaking down and cost me barely one-third the price of a new one. He asked, "Don't you pay all the utilities in that apartment complex you just bought?" Before the conversation was over, he'd gotten my attention. Only a few days later, while paying some electric bills at the power company, the person in line in front of me was returning a device available to all customers who paid a security deposit to check or measure electric usage. To make a long story short, I checked out the same device and within no time monitored the tons of money I was throwing in the air by retaining so many of those older-style refrigerators. At that time, most of the old refrigerators I had were consuming around $20 of electricity each per month, and I found out that most newer models cost less than half that to operate. Since I purchased a lot of second-hand models at that time, and still do, I quickly began to replace my very old models with other used models, but of a much higher efficiency rating.

My point here is obvious. We need to constantly remind ourselves that the high cost of energy is here to stay, and we must remain cognizant of as many ways as possible to cut energy costs. Even if you are a landlord who never pays any heating or cooling costs, or a single utility bill of any kind, you must realize the less utilities cost your tenants, the more rent you can ultimately charge.

As I've employed the term many times in this book, you can *scavenge*, or cut costs, the most by changing most of your major home appliances to higher efficiency models, whether they be new or used. Examples of those types of appliances, of course, are wall air conditioning units, central air conditioning units, furnaces, refrigerators, and water heaters.

While we're on the topic of energy savings, there are many other areas to scavenge costs. Lighting, for example, is an area where tremendous savings can be realized, both for interior as well as exterior usage. Many times at my apartment complexes, I've been able to cut the monthly electric bill in half, simply by putting some of the lighting on timers, by changing the light fixtures to accommodate the highest efficiency bulbs obtainable, and by keeping the electricity turned off in the empty apartments until they're reoccupied.

At one of the multifamily apartment complexes I purchased most recently in Texas, we were able to cut the monthly electric bill in half. That is, we reduced the portion of the electric usage the landlord or owner pays to illuminate the common areas such as interior hallways, the night lights set to a timer just outside each entrance door, and all the night lights that illuminate each of the more than 100 carports on the property.

Most of the light fixtures, needless to say, were obsolete and needed to be changed. Though the property owner, before I acquired the property, paid for this electrical usage, as I do now as the new owner, he thought he was saving money by letting each tenant change his or her own (old-style incandescent) bulb each time they needed to be replaced. What he failed to realize was shocking to me. For one thing, tenants were screwing into the light sockets anywhere from 15-watt to 200-watt bulbs, mostly all incandescent types. For another thing, only a small handful of those light fixtures had been converted to a modern type of fixture.

Upon possession of the property, we immediately updated all the lighting in these common areas. The dusk-to-dawn entry and patio lantern, distributed by Cooper Lighting, LLC. of Peachtree City, Georgia, was the perfect fit for more than 90% of our needs. This exterior lamp, made by Sylvania and marketed by many home improvement stores, has its own built-in sensor, sells for somewhere in the $13 range on sale, and comes with a 13-watt fluorescent bulb that lasts an average of 9 years and has an output of 60 watts! Is it any wonder we cut our electric bill in half?

Other scavengable ways to save energy are by doing the following:

- Monitoring water heater setting
- Installing programmable thermostats
- Installing low E thermopane windows
- Installing insulated entrance and exit doors
- Installing quality blinds and drapes
- Applying weather stripping
- Installing ceiling, sidewall, and roof insulation

Just last week my office manager and I reviewed some utility bills. Suddenly it occurred to us that among three of my 24-unit apartment buildings, all in a row, all consisting of two-bedroom units with the exact same square footage in each, that the gas bill for the middle building was exceedingly high. As we studied the situation, we noted the monthly gas bill in that one building was averaging about $300 more than the other two buildings in the colder months and about $200 more during the warmer months. Within an instant, I had Wayne, my apartment manager at that location, on the telephone, and said to him, "Check the water heater settings at each of the three buildings, and call me right back."

Within 10 minutes, Wayne reported to me that the water heaters in the two end buildings were set at 110 degrees, while the water heater in the middle building was set at 125 degrees. Though no logical explanation could be found, look at the ton of money I was losing until last week just on one water heater!

Before I get to scavenging the cost of water and water consumption, let me comment on the importance of taking the time to get multiple bids before contracting labor or services. Taking extra bids is of *great importance*! Why? Because almost 100% of the time, you can find another company, contractor, or laborer, with as much or more experience, with a good reputation, with lower overhead, and, for whatever reason, who charges somewhat less to a lot less. What was it that ol' Ben Franklin said? Wasn't it, "A penny saved is a penny earned"? Except in many cases, nowadays, we're talking about hundreds, thousands, and, in some cases, tens of thousands of dollars saved! So when finding out what something is going to cost, even though the first person you talk to might sound extraordinarily truthful and overly convincing, do yourself a big favor and get a variety of bids. Also, not only that, but take the extra time to allow those people to educate you to the utmost on the topic at hand. You will be glad you did!

If you own any kind of business, or if you're in the housing industry, unless you have the ability to perform any of these serious tasks in-house, consider getting multiple bids on labor and services such as these:

- Telephone, Internet, and fax services
- Laundry services
- Cable or satellite service
- Trash collection
- Snow removal
- Insurance
- Landscaping
- Cleaning
- Book-keeping
- Plumbing
- Painting
- Pest control
- Paving and/or seal coating
- HVAC
- Electrical
- Flooring
- Roofing
- Carpentry
- Concrete work

Before ending this chapter, another very important category that we constantly need to remind ourselves of is how to scavenge or curtail the cost of water, or "liquid gold," as I commonly like to say. If there ever was a survey done around the world, asking people if they thought their water bills were too high, I have absolutely no doubt that the vast majority of people would respond with a resounding *yes*, that their water bills were definitely too high. So why, then, don't more of us take the initiative and reduce the amount of water we use? The truth of the matter is that until relatively recently, we didn't have as many water-saving options available to us. However, thanks to modern inventions for the most part, by employing certain techniques, we can greatly reverse the rising cost of water, mainly by cutting consumption. At most businesses having anything to do with plumbing, and particularly at home improvement stores such as Lowe's, Menards, Home Depot, and so forth, you usually will be able to find water-saving products. The most common products to help curtail water consumption are as follows:

- Low-flow shower heads
- Aerators for faucets
- Toilet tank banks, sometimes called bladders
- Standard 1.6-gallon flush toilets
- Duel flush toilets
- Flapperless toilets

When it comes to water-consumption products, I recently found a company on the Internet that seems to have an answer for our every need, with very attractive prices. We've been pleased to do business with Conservation Warehouse in the Philadelphia area, telephone number 800-875-2955. While ordering a large quantity of low-flow shower heads that allow only 1.5 gallons per minute (GPM) at $4.50 plus a large quantity of toilet bladders for $1.13 each, we discovered three unique types of water-saver toilets.

1. The Ecologic, which was 1.28 gallons per flush (GPF), is made by Niagara and is also called the Flapperless toilet; it can be bought in the $120 range if orders are of a minimum of several dozen units. This toilet is known as the favorite among owners of hotels, motels, and apartment complexes.
2. Another recommended toilet handled by Conservation Warehouse and also made by Niagara is the Power One. This toilet uses only 1.0 GPF and can be bought in large orders for under $140 per toilet.
3. The third recommended toilet, also made by Niagara and known as the Stealth, requires only 0.8 GPF and can be purchased in large bulk orders for about $143 per toilet.

Since surveys nationwide show that 26.7% of all household water usage goes through the toilet, and unless you can afford to do almost a daily walk-through of each of your bathrooms, having nonleaking, very efficient toilets is a very strong consideration this day and age.

So, how much water do we really use? I found the following statistics interesting. Hopefully they will be interesting to you as well. Most surveys in the United States show indoor water usage as follows:

1. 26.7% from toilets
2. 21.7% from clothes washers
3. 16.8% from showers
4. 15.7% from faucets
5. 13.7% from leaks
6. 3% from other uses

Key Points

- Replace old inefficient appliances and lighting with newer, more efficient devices. Newer devices will keep your electrical, gas, and water bills down.
- Install energy-efficient windows and doors.
- Replace inefficient furnaces, air conditioners, and water heaters.
- Seek multiple bids on all labor and services you can't perform yourself.
- Monitor sudden increases in water, gas, or electrical use and their causes.

Ten

Scavenging the Loopholes,
Incentives, and Rebates

In this chapter, I will try to inspire you and make you more aware of the fairly significant amounts of money out there, practically just waiting for you in the form of gifts to claim—"money just waiting for the taking," as my dad used to say. Though I have to admit this chapter was definitely not first and foremost on my mind when I began to outline *Scavenge Your Way to Real Estate Riches*, its significance is paramount in the overall scheme of things, as I will show you.

Loopholes

Though countless types of loopholes exist that greatly benefit you financially, depending to some degree on your particular city, state, or region, in this chapter I've chosen to describe only four different categories. They are co-ops, property tax protests, utility sales tax exemptions, and tax abatements.

A housing co-op can be formed in some states, for example, and may reduce property taxes by as much as 50%. This is something I've done on two occasions, as I'll explain shortly. A co-op in this sense allows people to simply rent, rather than own stake, in the co-op. It allows an apartment complex to be run as a nonprofit entity and for the reduction in taxes to go back into renovating or maintaining this complex. Knowing all of your states' regulations on these co-ops is important, though. Some allow the payouts from these properties to be only in the forms of wages to managers and other employees, but not paid directly to the owners.

For a large property that will require many renovations over a long period of time, this may be ideal as lower taxes would lower overhead and shorten the renovation time frame, as more money could be put into it. Once all the renovations are complete, there's almost nothing to say you can't sell the whole thing to someone else who, in turn, would run it as a corporation "for profit" and be able to demonstrate a huge gain in value of the property.

Just five short years ago, I created my first co-op in Des Moines, Iowa, upon purchasing a 108-unit complex. As luck would have it, I'd just invited my friend Rich for coffee, anxious to tell him about an apartment complex I might purchase. As we were saying good-bye, he said, "Steve, will you convert it to a co-op?" I said, "A co-op?" I had barely heard the word before and knew nothing about the benefits I could create for myself. When Rich mentioned being able to cut my property taxes in half, I immediately took notice! To make a long story short, I now pay roughly $70,000 per year in property taxes, instead of paying roughly $140,000, on that 108-unit complex. What would have been a so-so deal turned into a very stable property, showing great appreciation in value.

Now that I've told you just how dramatic certain loopholes can be if you bother to take advantage of them, particularly in converting a ordinary apartment complex into a "not for profit" co-op, please take my advice and investigate the advantages available to you in your area.

Property Tax Protests

Another loophole you should investigate comes in the form of trying to reduce your property taxes by protesting them. Of course, this is something you or someone in your corporation can do, but most entities that own property in larger cities choose to hire a company or law office that specializes in this kind of work. Most states have all the forms and instructions online, however, if you or your company is "do it yourself" minded.

Since owning some large apartment complexes in the Houston area, I have hired a company to protest my taxes at each location and have now just received the results. On my 150-unit complex, I received an astounding $21,000 annual property tax reduction! Among the various companies that will protest your taxes, in the Houston area, for instance, at least 15 companies have contacted me by letter, offering their services. In case you might be wondering if the rate charged varies from company to company, the answer is a resounding yes. Among those 15 or so companies that contacted me, a wide range of commissions were sought, from 15% to 35% of the actual dollar amount they are able to reduce your taxes for the upcoming year. In other words, their commission, or percentage charged, does not carry over to following years. As a further tidbit of information, only one of those 15 or so companies did not base their charges on a percentage and instead asked for a flat dollar amount per property.

To give you an example, just from one year to the next, from 2011 to 2012, the actual dollars I paid for property tax on one of my properties increased from about $58,000 to around $66,000. So, if the company you choose charges you 25%, and they are able to cut the increase from $8,000 down to $4,000, the company would receive $1,000 for having helped you get your taxes reduced.

Utility Sales Tax Exemption

On a smaller scale, you can also look into tax-exempt status on some expenses such as lighting. This can be highly variable, and even the same state might have different rules from city to city, such as in the example I'm about to give you. Some cities allow for lighting used in common areas, like hallways, the club house, the office, and so forth, to be exempt from taxes, while some do not.

For example, the lighting in the common areas at my one property in Pasadena, Texas, is tax exempt. On the other hand, at another property I own in Houston, less than seven miles away, the lighting there is not given tax-exempt status. Depending on the size of your property, simply applying for this tax-exempt status can save you from a few hundred to a few thousand dollars each year.

Often a state will require a utilities study to determine just how much is exempt. Several services exist for this, as well, similar to the companies that will protest your taxes for you. If you're new to the area where you've made your purchase, a few simple phone calls made early on will undoubtedly result in a very significant savings for you.

Tax Abatements

To help reduce property rehab start-up costs, many cities throughout the United States offer tax abatement programs. Going back a number of years, I recall going out of my way to "not" sign up for certain tax abatements that were available to me, fearing that the city, later on, would increase my taxes by a disproportional amount because of my improvements. However, looking back on it, I clearly would have been more money ahead to have taken advantage of those abatements I refused.

The city of Des Moines, Iowa, for example, offers tax abatements. New additions and renovations of less than $40,000 are eligible for an 115% abatement for 10 years. Also, new construction and rehab projects of more than $40,000 are eligible for abatements of 100% over 5 years.

Still, other cities are a bit more conservative, such as the city of St. Louis, Missouri. There, new construction on vacant land or a gut rehabilitation of an existing building is eligible for a property tax abatement lasting 5 to 10 years. During that period, the property tax rate is frozen at the value of the property before the improvements. In any event, tax abatements can save you money, which is the bottom line, and should be taken advantage of as you prosper in real estate and as you gain equity and build your net worth.

Incentives

Weatherization

Common subsidies exist throughout most communities to either directly or indirectly benefit the tenant, as well as the landlord/investor. For example, here in the Midwest, subsidies exist to help keep housing and utility costs down. One such program, known as Mid-Iowa Community Action, or MICA, is set up to weatherize housing units. Though you, as a landlord, may have to sign an agreement stating that you won't sell the property until a few years have passed, or that you won't terminate the lease of a low-income tenant without just cause, the monetary benefits to the property and to the landlord can be tremendous and can be had merely by filling out a tiny bit of paperwork.

So, what does this program, MICA, do to the property, in the form of weatherization (at no charge to the landlord, mind you)? Well, for one, they insulate a number of areas, including attics, sidewalls, and crawlspaces. If the property needs a new furnace simply because the present one is of a lower efficiency rating, a new furnace will be installed. Other details undertaken "for free" are the weather stripping of door, and exterior caulk work, including caulking around windows and other common areas. If your attic isn't vented properly, new attic vents will be installed, and even minor masonry repairs are done to foundations. Though the list goes on and on, one last thing I'll mention is that this program will even build ramps to improve wheelchair accessibility. An example of such a program is described at www.micaonline.org/housing.

Section 8

In case you're unaware, the Section 8 program assists eligible people by paying a portion of their rent to a private owner. This program is funded by the Department of Housing and Urban Development (HUD) and applied by your state housing development agency (human resource or city housing agency). Section 8 applicants' gross annual income must fall below the income limits set by HUD, and they generally seem to be single mothers, the elderly, and/or disabled people.

Though there are positives and negatives with this program and with some tenants, in my opinion, the advantages are much in the favor of the investor who has C level housing and who rents to low- and moderate-income tenants. So, what is the upside of having Section 8 tenants?

First of all, the government always pays its bills on time and currently will even electronically deposit your rent check into your bank account on the first of each month. Also, these tenants tend to stay through the end of their rent contract and renew their rent contract more often than the average tenant, meaning they tend to stay put. Also, these tenants are more likely to accept an apartment that otherwise is fine but lacks curb appeal to the average tenant. And, if these tenants like your place, many others very soon tend to find you.

As far as the negatives are concerned, sometimes there is a bit more rent loss, waiting on the paperwork to get done. Also, there is always an extra amount of paperwork compared to a "regular" tenant. Further, sometimes there are paperwork processing delays, and, last, the property has to be inspected once every year, instead of every three years, as would be the case for municipal inspections in most communities. The prospect of tenants who tend to stay put, combined with the fact that your rent check is guaranteed to arrive on the first of each month, should be convincing enough evidence that Section 8 offers you more stability as a property owner.

Lead Abatement

Even though lead was removed from paints in the late 1970s except for industrial purposes, you still need to be aware of this topic and how the lead abatement program can benefit you as a property owner. Almost all investors in real estate take an older property at least once, early in our investing careers. If that property was built before 1978, there's a very high probability that lead paint was used there, especially if the woodwork, such as door trim, window trim, baseboards, and so on, was painted instead of stained and varnished. Since the lead in lead-based paint adds a sweet flavor to it, and because little kids tend to put all sorts of things in their mouths, including paint chips, lead poisoning occurs. Because lead is considered toxic waste and workers removing it need to be suited up, use special tools, and be specially trained, the costs can be considerably high.

This is why lead abatement subsidies exist and why HUD and local governments issue lead abatement grants for the purpose of taking some of the sting out of the expense.

How can this benefit you as a property owner? First of all, the word *grant* means gift. Though I personally have not applied for a lead abatement grant, many people I know have, and some have been recipients. These types of grants can be as much as $25,000 on one of your properties, even though the rental property owner is required to pay 10% of the cost. There's some paperwork involved, but what the heck? This means you can scavenge a whole remodel job, you can increase rents, and you can gain lots more money when you get around to selling the property. All this for only 10% of the cost, and by filling out the forms and jumping through a few hoops! Check with your local government agencies to see if this grant money is available in your area. For further information, go to www. portal.hud.gov/hudportal/hud.

Decorating

Before I finish this segment on incentives, several more things deserve mentioning as they either financially benefited me or someone close to me.

Several years ago, soon after taking possession of the 108-unit complex I own in Des Moines, I received a call from Jetz Companies, Inc. The caller said something like, "Congratulations on your purchase, Steve. This is Don from Jetz, and I'd like to talk to you about renewing your laundry contract with us and about a very handsome decorating allowance we can offer you." Before then, I'd never ever heard of a decorating allowance. I remember asking him, "Did I hear you say something about an allowance?"

To make a long story short, I soon signed a 10-year extension of my laundry contract and received a total of $32,100, just for my signature on a piece of paper. By the way, this contract, still in effect, gives me 50% of all money taken in by the washers and dryers in the laundry rooms of the property, and I don't have to mess with the machines in any way. In other words, I don't have to worry about repairs if there is destruction from vandalism, if the machines naturally break down, if they need to be replaced, if the money is removed in a timely manner without the coin boxes overflowing, and so on. Though it can be argued that more profit exists if you service the machines yourself, I still made the right decision for myself at the time. As some of you own or will own larger apartment complexes, think of how big your decorating allowance would be with Jetz, or companies like them, if your complexes were double or triple the size of my 108-unit complex!

Something else you can do to put handsome sums of money in your pocket, if you have apartment complexes, is to contact the satellite companies in your area that provide Internet and television service.

Just recently I had a conversation with my new manager in Houston. She said, "Steve, there's something you really need to check out." As I asked her to explain, she said, "My old boss signed a seven-year contract with one of the satellite companies to rewire five complexes and received a bonus of ten thousand dollars for each one, totaling fifty thousand dollars!" I said, "Wow, that's a pretty good 'day's pay.' Why don't we investigate since I have two large complexes less than seven miles apart?" She said, "Steve, I've already placed the call for you."

As this segment comes to an end, my advice to you is to always keep your eyes and ears open and pay attention to what others are saying. You may even be able to generate more income by placing soda machines, snack machines, video machines, and so on at some of your properties. A friend of mine told me about a vending machine on the market that sells frozen treats that's making its owner a nice bit of money, an idea that just might be worth checking out. In closing, let me tell you about a friend who is lucky enough to have a tall building near the center of my hometown. The cell phone companies far and wide have "found him" and as a result have earned him upward of a million dollars per year for the past several years. Since so many investors are interested in buying out the contacts he has with various cell phone companies, he's gotten really good at playing one bid against the other, creating even bigger profits for himself. This kind of "luck" will come your way, too, the harder you work and the more vigilant you are.

Energy

Energy costs have risen by over 20% in the last decade, more than three times the average rent increases and easily surpassing property tax and homeowners insurance costs.

Multifamily dwellings in the United States, most with an average age of 36 years, can potentially save an estimate $9 billion in energy costs.

Opportunities exist for responsible, proactive owners to market superior energy efficiency to prospective tenants by better communicating how their properties consume less energy and by making energy-efficient investments.

If energy-efficient commercial buildings in the United States have higher rental and occupancy rates, why not multifamily residential properties?

One easy place to get started is by requesting your electricity and natural gas usage data from your respective service provider and doing some basic analysis.

For example, in June 2012, I was approached by a consultant who identified a natural gas savings opportunity at one of my rental properties down in Houston, Texas.

Texas has a deregulated natural gas market, and by signing a one-year natural gas sales agreement with a competitive supplier, I was able to recover over $8,000 of a previously made deposit and reduce the premium I paid for each unit of natural gas by almost 50%.

One should also consider the actual meters; more often than not, a meter that is not showing obvious problems or leaks will just be left in place for decades. The original calibration may possibly have skewed considerably over time to the point where you could be paying too much for your gas. Of course, if the error is in your favor, the new meter won't be doing you any favors.

Of course, you want to compare between buildings, both your own and others in the area similar to yours, to try and estimate if your readings are skewing high or low.

We discovered at one of the Texas properties, by means of some very basic benchmarking, comparing natural gas usage by square foot between two relatively comparable properties, that a meter was not working correctly. Once the problem was solved and invoices restarted, I was able to recover several thousand dollars.

Many deregulated states have websites that you can visit to compare rates. In Texas, I would recommend visiting Power to Choose (www.powertochoose.org) and TrueCost Electric Portal (www.mytruecost.com). When choosing a plan, make sure that you understand the total cost and not just the price per kilowatt hour.

Getting back to energy efficiency, here are just a few of an immense list of opportunities:

- Ensure that all equipment is functioning as designed.
- Purchase Energy Star qualified appliances.
- Install vending machine controllers.
- Optimize elevators for occupancy variations.
- Lower swimming pool and hot tub temperature settings.

Rebates

In this section we'll discuss three different types of rebates, as well as tax credits. Even though they are different than rebates, tax credits are discussed here to limit the great number of subtopics, keeping the information more concise, easier to understand, and less confusing.

Among the various types of rebates that exist, I've determined that these three types will do the most to help you, as investors, or even if you own nothing more than your residence as a single-family dwelling.

First of all, you should be aware why rebates exist. The government, utility companies, and other interests are glad to freely spend by giving rebates, as energy demand increases, to be able to cut back on the hundreds of billions of dollars needed to improve infra-structure every decade or so, to build more power-generation capac-ity, or drill more gas wells, and so forth.

Three of the most common types of rebates that will help you the most are material supplier rebates, utility rebates, and manufacturers rebates.

Material supplier rebates are given out by offering you cash back,usually if you use that company's credit card, and if you buy a certain minimal dollar amount, sometimes by a certain date. For example, many companies such as Home Depot, Lowe's, Menards, Grainger, and so on offer you as much as a 5% cash back rebate, sometimes on select purchases, yet at other times on everything in the store. While you're at it, don't forget about smaller rebates such as the 2% available to you at places like Costco, which at the same time may offer you a reduced cost for other items such as gasoline.

However, far more significant than 5% are rebates from utility com-panies or certain energy-saver appliances. If you soon plan to replace a major item such as a furnace or central air conditioner, hundreds of dollars in rebates await you if the air conditioner is above a cer-tain Service Energy Efficiency Rating (SEER)number, such as 16, and the furnace is above certain efficiency rating in percent, such as 90% or higher. Take a moment to talk to an installer in your area or call your local utility company to ask about rebates. You'll be glad you did.

Another type of rebate available at times comes from the company that manufactures the product. This type of rebate is less common but does exist from time to time, usually to get rid of older models to make room in warehouses for the newest or latest models. Always ask before you buy. Just think of how large companies such as Ford and General Motors coerce us every year with *huge* rebates if we hurry up and buy a car or truck by a certain date, before the shipment of next year's models arrive. Smaller companies selling air conditioners, and so forth, do the same thing. You just have to look around. Before leaving this topic, let me briefly mention that my hometown of Marshalltown, Iowa, is the home of Lennox Industries, a large worldwide manufacturer of furnaces, central air conditioners, and so on. Just last year Lennox offered a $300 rebate on a certain type of furnace for a certain period of time. Though I didn't take advantage of that offer, someone like you or I very easily could have. Just stay in the know and you'll discover these same types of rebates in your area.

Last, let me mention tax credits. This differs from a rebate in that you don't get any money back, but you do get the amount you pay in taxes reduced. For example, let's say that after filing your taxes, your accountant determines you owe the federal government $2,000. However, because the government offers an energy tax credit of $300 on a particular type of furnace you bought during the taxable year, the actual amount you would owe in federal taxes would be only $1,700, not $2,000. Take a moment to Google the Energy Star program to see just how many different ways these tax credits can help you.

Key Points

- Co-ops can provide a great reduction in tax burdens.
- Protest your property's assessed value to reduce taxes.
- Use tax abatements to reduce taxes while renovating properties.
- Search for low-income resident subsidies to improve the building's energy efficiency and overall value.
- Seek out Section 8 tenants to keep your lower-grade properties full and generating income.

Eleven

Scavenging the Internet

The following links should give you some idea of what's available when looking for resources online. When in doubt, visit Google and try your luck by refining your search terms and location.

www.habitat.org/restore

ReStores have used and occasionally new materials. These stores are all over the United States. They can be a great place to pick up all sorts of cheap odds and ends for a restoration project when you're on a tight budget.

Material suppliers will donate scratch-and-dent items and materials to these stores for tax credits. Contractors will often unload excess materials they don't need after a build and then pick up other materials they might need later on.

The ReStores also have tool libraries for the use of members, who can check out a particular tool needed rather than having to buy it.

www.northsidematerialbrokers.com

A good example of a closeout warehouse is Northside Material Brokers out of Atlanta, Georgia. Georgia produces a large amount of building materials, and this store seems to have a bit of everything.

They advertise one of the largest assortments of countertops in the Southeastern Unites States.

Items in inventory include kitchen cabinets, doors, countertops, recessed lighting, exterior doors, landscaping products, shingles, and surplus, salvage, blemished, scratch-and-dent, or overstock discount merchandise.

While the focus mainly seems to be on kitchen renovation and exterior doors, they also have much in the way of seasonal items and assortments of random surplus materials.

www.buildersdiscount.net

Farther north is Builders Discount Center, with chains in the North Carolina area. The selection is a bit more modest and typical of the hit-and-miss nature of such businesses.

Their main focus seems to be on windows, siding, shingles, and lumber, but they also have a large selection of cabinets, kitchen sinks, and molding.

www.secondsandsurplus.com

This store has an emphasis on kitchens, bathrooms, and flooring, with a wide selection of all.

Often a building materials store will try to have everything A–Z or else a limited selection with a wider array of products. This site mainly appears to be an interior remodeling supplier.

Stores such as this, with a name like Seconds and Surplus, may have established connections with factories and various warehouses specializing in the intended core market.

www.craigslist.com

Check Craigslist mainly under "materials" for sale to find builder surplus. This is the place to find everything from used to excess materials in most communities.

As Craigslist does not represent a store, but the community sales trends at large, you have to be on the lookout for different products in different seasons. Going into winter, probably all exterior building materials will be on sale.

After winter, people like to unload their entire supply of unused pavers, gardening items, fence posts, chainsaws, and wood stoves. The latter two seem to relate to people who think they will save big that first winter but rapidly get sick of cutting wood, stacking wood, and loading wood.

During winter, you'll see a lot of water heaters, old furnaces, lawn tractors, baseboard heaters, and surplus insulation on sale. Most of this is renovation excess for people discovering that their house isn't ready for winter.

Sites For New Material

www.americanbuildersurplus.com

American Builder Surplus is a place where contractors and builders unload various items so they don't have to store them or throw them away. Prices can be quite reasonable, but the items available vary day to day.

This place is somewhat of a scavenger hunt in itself as you select your region and what you're looking for. Some regions of the United

States also are not as active as others, but the site is certainly worth a look if you're in a part of the country with more active participation.

www.diggerslist.com

This site covers just about everything under the sun, including building materials, patio furniture, tools, filing cabinets, and storage buildings. Enter your zip code and a mileage radius and you're ready to start hunting.

www.buildersupplyoutlet.com

This business is more focused on flooring, kitchens, and bathroom materials. The materials are mainly overstocks, overruns, and discontinued items.

The savings are considerable even if the selection is a bit hit and miss sometimes. They have locations in Chicago, Texas, Kentucky, and Georgia.

www.builderelements.com

This store has a wide selection of tiles, as well as bathroom and kitchen remodeling supplies. While they have factory direct prices, they have many decorative items that would shock the "go big or go home" crowd.

It's certainly worth a look if you have a hard-to-please customer or just to see what's possible and what is out there. Metallic glass tile, quartz tile, granite tile, stainless steel tile, and a number of tiles there have to be seen to be believed.

Their selection of laminate and engineered hardwood flooring is also worth a look.

They have their showroom in Las Vegas, Nevada, but they will ship just about anywhere in Europe or North America. If you want to create the ultimate "show-off" home, this is the place to go before all the rest.

www.empiresurplus.com

Empire Surplus Home Center has a wide variety of closeouts, buybacks, and liquidation items. In addition, the stores have a wide selection of home renovation items as well as furniture.

The widest selection for this store seems to be in its selection of cabinets, faucets, and furniture items. Also of interest are the hot tubs available.

Based out of Leesport, Pennsylvania, Empire is another good example of a regional discount home renovation store.

www.builddirect.com

This place does mostly decking, flooring, siding, and paving. They have everything you need for an indoor and outdoor renovation of your property. The selection is pretty wide, and they also include a good selection of "how-to" articles in the Learning Section.

BuildDirect will ship anywhere in North America.

www.knoxrailsalvage.com

Knoxville Rail Salvage is mostly building materials. It has a limited selection of various items, all deeply discounted from retail prices.

While most people are not familiar with railroad salvage stores, you should consider using them. Railroads and shipping companies often have mishaps. A pallet will break, something will fall off the edge of the loading dock, or, worse, tons of cargo will dump out when someone opens the door to the rail car or truck trailer.

The shipper will then try to sell off the undamaged remains for whatever they can. As the accidents are random, so are the items likely to be damaged and sold off at a more generic rail salvage store.

Check Google to find a local salvage place, or call your local railroad or shipping company to find out where they sell their salvage.

www.amiparts.com and *www.mcmelectronics.com* (under "appliance parts")

When you're buying closeout appliances, the biggest risk is not being able to find replacement parts. These are two of the companies that buy up old appliance parts for sales to repairmen and techs. AMI supplies mainly microwave parts and some other appliance odds and ends. MCM Electronics has a wide selection of manufacture and generic replacement parts for appliances as well as consumer electronics.

Also of interest is the selection of test equipment, network and cable wiring, home security products, home theater equipment, and satellite TV products.

Resources for Construction Items and Home Improvement Topics

www.reddit.com/r/DIY

This "sub-reddit" covers an assortment of do-it-yourself projects, from small craft items to full-blown home renovations.

If you have questions, create an account and ask them here.

There's plenty of advice on the most common projects as well as some of the more off-the-wall ones.

Many people also show off their latest projects and help other people with theirs when they get stuck or run out of ideas.

www.diychatroom.com

This site covers every imaginable home improvement topic. They're laid out differently than reddit and support picture and video postings in the forum.

This may work much better for those who are more visual and less computer adept as you don't have to open up a dozen browser tabs to follow the train of conversation.

This site may appeal to a more specific DIY and crafting crowd as it's not part of a much larger forum dealing with countless other subjects.

www.ascentergy.com

Provides cost savings related to energy needs.

Located in the Houston area, the company helps lower energy costs.

www.homepower.com

This site focuses mostly on renewable energy and technical aspects of various technologies. The site features articles and longer publications for free.

Want to learn how to set up a solar heating solution for your pool? This is the place to go. They also cover a number of topics relating to improving home efficiency and reducing your power expenses, such as microhydro power, photovoltaic power systems, wind power, passive solar home design, improving home efficiency, biofuels, and hybrid cars.

As energy prices continue to increase over the years, the subject materials on this site become more and more important.

www.motherearthnews.com

These editors and writers always seem to have something useful to say about topics such as green housing, renewable energy, gardening, and DIY projects.

Country living, green building materials, urban gardening, rainwater collection, and flowerbed composting are some of the many topics covered here.

This is the great-granddaddy, or great-grandmother, of greener living technology publications.

www.backwoodshome.com

This site is for those who really want to get away from it all: where there is no grid, just a whisper of cell phone access, and certainly no broadband access. Helpful for those looking to restore great great-grandad's cabin in rural Idaho, Alaska, or some other no man's land.

Backwoods Home covers some construction techniques that are generally forgotten but that are practical when the closest hardware store may be five hours away or more or closed until spring.

Be sure to visit this site well before you venture out into "parts unknown."

www.youtube.com

www.youtu.be/FQvFzdFlp08 (the basic lay
ers of home construction)

In addition to offering a quick overview of how homes are built, YouTube also covers countless other topics such as construction, green building, deconstruction, architectural salvage, staging, and just about anything someone can imagine.

If you can dream it up, someone else may have shot video of it already. If not, make your own video, upload it, and see if you can't attract a following. This is the nature of what makes YouTube interesting, offering as it does professional video to amateur video and all levels in between—from the mundane to the outright unbelievable.

If YouTube doesn't have it, you can also try *Vimeo.com* or *Metacafe. com*.

Deals

www.fatwallet.com/blog

Coupons, sales, product deals, and free stuff, this site offers one-stop shopping for people looking to save money on a variety of retail purchases.

Now and again you just have to outright buy new things rather than scavenging them. If it comes down to that, pay a visit to this place and see if you can avoid paying full retail prices.

Investing and Finance

www.suzeorman.com

You can't afford it! OK, there's more to Suze than that. In addition to being a marketplace for her books and videos, this site provides a number of online calculators and resources for those looking to reign in their budgets, as well as information about wills, trusts, 401k and retirement accounts, insurance, mutual funds, stocks, bonds, and insurance.

Suze inspires you to be a little less spendthrift and quite a bit more thrifty. Your kids probably won't hate you that badly for not burning up hundreds every time you visit the mall or flying around to see every relative six times a year.

Saving up a bit of money, and forgetting about keeping up with the neighbors, isn't such a bad thing when the economy tanks, health care costs spike, and energy costs are on a roller coaster.

www.daveramsey.com

Dave is a bit like Suze, but with more coverage of real estate topics. He had online calculators, videos, links to buy his books, and all sorts of advice.

If you've got some money burning a hole in your pocket, maybe you just aren't satisfied with the bank's 0.42% money market payout, or possibly you've decided to stop your $120-a-week scratch-off ticket habit and have decided now is the time to try your hand at investing.

Dave Ramsey will give you the lay of the land in the field of investing and can help you build a road map for how you want to invest in the long-term or the short-term.

Real estate can be a good start, but it's always good to diversify your investments to hedge against the unpredictable.

www.money.msn.com/personal-finance

MSN money has up-to-the-minute news on the worlds of business and finance. It's worth a quick look every now and then if you invest a lot, if you are looking to see how the market is fluctuating, or if you wonder how much the government is likely to be picking your pocket in the next year.

This site also contains a lot of general big-picture stuff. Sometimes you can get new ideas on how to better refine your investment strategies by seeing what's going on outside your main field of operations.

Will the bedbug epidemic drive people away from dry cleaners and back to doing their own laundry, or does it simply spell the beginning of the end for furnished apartments?

Do your properties need Wi-Fi hotspots to keep the technology addicted from going to another property? Or will the 3G to 4G transition make Wi-Fi hotspots redundant?

It never hurts to keep your eyes open for new trends and marketing opportunities.

www.investopedia.com/personal-finance

Investopedia provides in-depth information on most financial and investment topics. If you need a bit more information than what's in the blog and on the news, this is the place to look around for a few hours.

Investopedia is a bit short of formal classes on topics, but the increased depth of knowledge compared to the usual media outlet sources is much better.

Active trading, investment strategies, how to clean up your credit, and market analysis are some interesting subjects covered here along with many others.

www.americasaves.org/savings-tips/finding-money-to-save

America Saves helps you look for all the small things in your life that tend to eat up a lot of money over time. Take a quick look around, and maybe you'll get a few new ideas.

How to save money, where to save money, what to save for, and other items of interest are here.

www.consumerismcommentary.com

An all around good "money site." Save money, invest money, make money. The site is somewhat spartan, but the articles on a variety of subjects are well written.

Examples of subjects covered are best online discount brokers, best credit cards, best mortgage interest rates, best online checking accounts, debt reduction, real estate, investing, and career topics.

www.johntreed.com/realestate.html

John Reed is most famous, and infamous, for his ratings of the real estate gurus. This is good for a quick look before you pay out $5,000–$19,000 for a seminar that amounts to fairy dust and wishful thinking.

His philosophy is more along the lines of "get rich slowly" rather than risking your credit, reputation, and jail time by trying to do a large number of high-risk and marginally legal real estate deals.

John Reed has a refreshing real-world perspective compared to many other authors who try to sell the improbable to impossible in the world of real estate. The site contains many freebies for those new to the real estate world and some good advice for the older ones who should have known better and are now trying to get a refund from a bogus "guru."

Legal Information

www.nolo.com

It's best to find a lawyer before you get into serious trouble. But for more routine things, you'll find out it pays to look around Nolo. Sometimes you just need the right document template, a signature or two, and a notary seal.

Some of their provided forms are these: Protect Your Trademark, File a Provisional Patent, Form a Limited Liability

Company, Use a Nondisclosure Agreement (NDA), Personal Forms, Create Your Will, Create Your Living Trust, Sign a Limited Power of Attorney for Finances, and Create a Promissory Note for Personal Loan.

Nolo also has a lot of general legal information as well. While it's not a replacement for a lawyer, it will reduce your need to use up a lawyer's time by doing some of the groundwork yourself.

www.legalzoom.com

LegalZoom is a step beyond Nolo. If you need the services of a lawyer or paralegal, the prices are right up front for a lot of common legal work.

Trademarks, LLC, copyrights, leases, and other contracts can be done through LegalZoom.

www.rocketlawyer.com

This is an online site for legal work that's a bit more involved than routine legal paperwork.

Immigration, personal injury, divorce, and so forth, RocketLawyer offers flat monthly rates for a number of services provided.

Do-It-Yourself Projects

www.instructables.com

This is a comprehensive DIY site. If you can imagine it, someone else has probably posted material on how to make it here. No project is too complex or off-the-wall here. Instructables contributors can help you think far out of the box if you need inspiration for some project you have in mind.

Instructables hosts electronics projects, workshop projects, and living, food, play, outdoors, and other types of projects.

www.lifehacker.com

Improve your life and live cheaper through creative thinking, savings, and use of technology. Lifehacker is similar to Instructables, but the articles are of somewhat less depth and not as step by step.

From unlocking your iPhone to unlocking the keys stuck in your car, the mundane to the outlandish are covered here on a daily basis. Many of these are helpful tips; others are just amusing or may help break you out of a creative rut or enable you to see a problem or routine task differently.

Global News and Finance

It is important to "stay in the know" by reading local and national newspapers, books, and magazines and keeping up to date via news outlets on the Internet.

A few good general sites to keep to get a sense of global news and finance are as follows:

www.ap.org/

www.cbc.ca/news/

www.bbc.co.uk/news/

www.reuters.com/

www.cbsnews.com/

www.consortiumnews.com

Money- and Business-Related Podcasts

www.brucewilliams.com

Bruce is rated in the top 100 all-time talk radio shows, and while he's no longer producing podcasts, much of the information he presents is still valid today. Bruce Williams hosted a show called "Your Money Matters" for many years and was an influence for many decades before all the other cable TV shows got in on the game.

www.castroller.com/podcasts/BiggerpocketsPodcast

and

www.biggerpockets.com/renewsblog/category/podcast

The Bigger Pockets podcast is ideal if you're trying to make that first million or your next millions. Many in-depth ideas are presented in these podcasts on a variety of subjects of interest to investors and businessmen.

Some of the subjects covered are aspects of landlording, house purchasing, flipping, investor psychology, financing strategies, wholesale real estate, and many others.

Organizations Specifically Geared toward Real Estate

www.american-apartment-owners-association.org

A fairly comprehensive site for the new landlord who needs links to everything.

You'll find do-it-yourself tips, tenant screening, discount insurance, inspection guides, real estate news, landlord legal forums, contractor discounts, books and software, vendor discounts, and many others.

www.agentfreebies.com

There are links to numerous free resources for realtors and real estate investors laid out in a one-page format. It's a good place to check out some links to get familiar with what's what in the field of real estate.

www.forbes.com/real-estate

This site offers coverage of the latest news in real estate if you feel the need to stay on top of the big picture. Most of the material covers general news as to what's going on in real estate and what's trending.

www.nationalreia.com

This is a good place for real estate investors and property owners to look around, get an idea of what the REIAs are about, and find a local chapter.

http://www.reiclub.com/real-estate-articles.php

At this site there are a huge number of real estate–related articles, videos, blogs, free books, and other things worth a look if you have a few hours or days to spare.

Included here are reviews of real estate audio books, e-books, seminars, and courses.

Investor resources include links to hard money lenders, real estate agents, handyman services, real estate clubs, business tools, and lists of state and federal laws.

There's also a link to forums on various topics related to real estate investment.

http://realestatecoursereviews.com

This site is worth a look before you drop $500 to $50,000 on a real estate course.

All the top latest favorites are reviewed on this site. Here you can get an idea of what the gurus of real estate really provide and what in their advertisements is mostly hot air or, worse, just a three-day-long commercial trying to sell you the "platinum package" and providing little to nothing more.

www.postlets.com

A one-stop site for advertizing your properties for rent or for sale. Tools on the site allow for syndication of the ad through affiliated publishers and social media outlets.

This is a useful tool if you need to fill vacancies in a tough market and need to keep your information out there for prospective clients.

www.backpage.com

Backpage provides free classifieds, somewhat similar to Craigslist.

Backpage has the advantage and disadvantage of being the new kid on the block. You might be one of the few for rent or for sale advertisers on the site, but you also have the problem of less eyeballs on the site every day.

The good news is that the price is right. Along with many of the other free sites on the Internet, you can widen your advertising footprint considerably by using these sites.

www.frontdoor.com

HGTVs website covers all things staging.

If you want your property to look like more than just another anonymous blank building, you need to furnish it to make it look like something someone could live in.

This site covers all the ins and outs for those who want to try their hand at staging.

www.loopnet.com

This free membership site covers real estate listings. The control panel makes it easy to get all the essential data on what you're looking for in an area of interest.

Key Points

- When in doubt, use Google, Bing, or Yahoo to determine whether a resource you need exists. Start with the key terms, and add more specific terms in later searches to narrow down what you need.
- Some sites have one or two good links to what you need; others have several hundred productive links.
- Sites with a limited advertising budget sometimes only update their Facebook or Twitter pages while their own website content is rarely updated. Be sure to check those sites for more up-to-the-minute news.
- You don't need to learn everything the hard way. Use Internet resources to "cheat" when you don't know how to do something.

Twelve

Scavenging the Rewards

Now that we've come to the end of this book, I just can't bring myself to say good-bye without helping you see the rewards, which also helps answer the question, "Why real estate?" Though I toyed with other titles for this chapter, such as "Gathering the Fruits," "Counting the Profits," or "Harvesting the Benefits," just in case you've ever wondered what goes through a writer's mind, I ultimately decided that "Scavenging the Rewards" seemed to be more encompassing, as you soon will be able to decide for yourself.

To some of us, the rewards might simply boil down to nothing more than being able to pursue real estate investing as a hobby. To others of us, the rewards we seek might only be finding peace of mind away from our full-time jobs or generating a small amount of passive income. Still, there are those of us who have even bigger expectations. By the time I bought my first rental property in 1977 at the age of 26, the only reward I had in mind was appreciation. After all, the word of the day was, "Buy, hold, and let the sucker appreciate." Everyone had me convinced that real estate prices would always be on the incline, despite occasional recessions, and for the most part they were right.

Generating Passive Income

Passive income is one of the many rewards you can expect once you start to invest in income property, and it refers to income received on a regular basis. It's derived from rents and from other business activities in which you do not materially participate, with little effort required to maintain it. In other words, after providing a tenant with a safe and comfortable place to stay, that passive income becomes your private ATM, constantly producing for you, whether you're close by or a long distance away, regardless of where you are or what you might be doing. What a tremendous feeling it is to experience this kind of reward, once you have your manager(s) and maintenance staff in place—to be able to live the lifestyle you choose and to monitor your passive income deposits and other business activity just by looking at a computer screen.

Passive income remains the envy of the highly educated professionals of our society, such as doctors, lawyers, dentists, and so on, who might enjoy very high incomes but still are stuck with the same ugly nemesis of the poor and uneducated. Though their income capacity can be very impressive, they still are stuck with having to trade time for money!

Quitting Your Full-Time Job

Another one of the rewards I refer to that you'll experience, especially if you're the least bit aggressive at investing in income property, is being able to quit your full-time job. There's no greater feeling than to be able to be your own boss, knowing that every ounce of effort you put forth is for your benefit, and not for that of someone else. As I like to say, when you reach this point in life, you realize that the other half of your brain is no longer being held hostage by the demands of your boss or by the demands of your employer. Being able to enjoy working around who you wish to work around, being able to enjoy great flexibility of schedule, being able to increase overall earning potential and be fully compensated, and being able to hire and fire as you see fit, without the threat of you yourself being fired or repri-manded, are only a very few of the many rewards that await you once you decide to be your own boss.

Retiring Early

Simply put, being able to retire early, in itself, is a huge advantage over someone who is forced to stay in the groove until reaching his or her midsixties. Of course you'll have to have enough passive income to be able to "retire early," but you won't have to worry about los-ing or not qualifying for certain retirement benefits, dictated by the one and only retirement plan your employer has put in place for you. Another reward connected to retiring early is that no one any longer places control over your time. In other words, you're completely in control of each day, all 24 hours of each and every day that passes. What a tremendous feeling it is to not have to wait for a retirement date on the calendar, to have enough money to pay your bills and to do the things you want without being straight-jacketed by someone else's schedule, pay grade, or plan for you to exit.

Being Financially Free

Being financially free is *the ultimate reward* that awaits you. All of a sudden your income level affords you the luxury of never having to work, or working only if you want to. Financial freedom will leave you much less stressed than before because the income is always there, remaining constant with little to no effort on your behalf.

You will have more energy for self-improvement. You also will gain a greater sense of purpose, you will stop looking for answers in the wrong places, and you will have more opportunities to think long-term. Thinking long-term can be beneficial for your investments, as well, because as your assets grow, the day-to-day market fluctuations will affect you less and less, which gives you the ability to take more risk for potentially higher returns.

Enjoying the Benefits of Appreciation

An increase or rise in the value of your property is known as appreciation. As I've already pointed out, the average yearly rate of inflation in the United States is around 5%. However, appreciation is inflation combined with investor demand and supply of availability. Therefore, your property values will appreciate at least as fast as the rate of inflation, and if you have any luck, at least a few percentage points more.

Just stop and think for a moment about the financial rewards of owning property that increases in value over time. For one thing, your monthly payments and interest rate should remain frozen for at least 10 years, if not for the life of the mortgage, all while your monthly rents collected will increase at roughly the same rate as inflation.

Looking at it from a different prospective, 10 years after taking out a mortgage on a rental property, your rents should be approximately 50% higher, while your P&I payment will have remained the same. Also, during that same 10-year period, your property will have increased in value by at least 50%. Now, stop dead in your tracks for a minute and answer me this question. How much interest would your down-payment money of 20% have generated for you during that same 10-year period, at a measly annual rate of 1% to 3%? In round figures, the difference would be like comparing a handful of cash to a truckload of cash, no ifs, ands, or buts! Though many more rewards can be scavenged from the benefits of appreciation, including harvesting huge tax shelters, and so on, let's move on to the next topic that stands all alone, also made available as a result of appreciation.

Enjoying Nontaxable Loan Proceeds

A very common practice of all types of investors, from your real estate tycoons or moguls all the way down to your low-income poor relation living in a two-bedroom bungalow on the other side of the tracks, is to pull a bunch of cash out of a property each time you refinance. This is sometimes referred to as "free money" because it's not counted as income, and not a single penny of income tax has to be paid on the amount of cash pulled out of the deal.

What a terrific feeling it is to know that you can extract a boatload of cash every few years, even from the same property, over, and over, and over again, never having to pay tax on that money, depending on how much each property appreciates, of course. The only negative is that it causes your payment to go up because the amount borrowed has increased. The only exception to that would be unless your previous interest rate before refinancing was higher than normal and if your new interest rate after refinancing was lower than normal. Then, as I've experienced, depending upon the length of your new loan, you just might see a drop in the actual amount of your monthly payment or payback rate. Isn't this just about the most absolutely incredible thing you've ever heard in your entire life?

About the middle of 2010, I purchased a large complex in Des Moines, Iowa, on a land contract, agreeing to pay the note within 16 months—by December 31, 2011. Upon refinancing through a local bank and paying off the owner, because of the equity I created by buying it right, combined with some rehab improvements due to the property suffering from deferred maintenance, I was able to pull $224,420.40 out of the property barely one year after having made the purchase.

Did you hear that? Would someone out there show me a better, quicker, cleaner, more legal way to produce a ton of cash? If that's not an example of the world's biggest scavengable reward connected to being an investor in real estate, then I'd really like to know what is!

Possessing Notable Treasures

Once you reach that passive income plateau from all your investment properties, there are many more types of rewards that await you. Have you ever heard the expression, "The only difference between men and boys is the price of their toys"? Though most of us like to have in our possession at least something that is slightly astounding, others of us like possessing things that bring out the wonderment, if not total astonishment, of others.

Therefore, the more "monopoly money" we have to spend, the higher the probability is that we amount and accumulate notable treasures. So, just what are these notable treasures? Of course you know that the list would go on indefinitely simply because what's considered valuable to one person would not be considered notable to another, and so on.

However, the more precious, antique, scarce, rare, or ancient something is, the more it's considered to be of higher value, right? OK, so what would be examples of some of these notable treasures that we, with monopoly money, tend to possess? How about ancient firearms, paintings, antique cars, vintage guitars, rare coins, unusual pieces of furniture, sculptures, precious metals such as gold and silver, jewelry, and so forth?

Even though at present I only possess rare coins and unusual wooden objects, other rewards that I plan to bestow upon myself are not far away. If you haven't started collecting notable treasures yet, it's important at least to go ahead and get your want list started. You have my permission. If you believe, as I do, that getting rich is only a matter of positioning yourself to be rich, then putting your hands on rare, valued, collectable, or sought-after treasures, likewise, is only a matter of you positioning yourself to do so!

Taking Extended Vacations

As has been true for a long time, those of us that can afford to do so use travel as a form of recreation and as a change of scenery to reenlighten or reinvigorate ourselves, apart from it being another way to enjoy life. Going back even 150 years and before, people with the means to do so moved to cooler climates during the warmer part of the year and to warmer climates during the cooler part of the year.

Even in the 1860s, president Abraham Lincoln spent his summers, for a few months at a time, in upper New England, having traveled there by horse and buggy, to escape the hot, humid summers of Washington, DC. Speaking from experience, though my wife and I haven't yet purchased a lakeside cabin in Minnesota or Canada to enjoy cooler summers, we definitely can proclaim just how great our extended vacations are at our winter house in south Texas. What a treat it is to not have to fight the bitter cold winters of the upper Midwest!

Having the means to travel is one thing, but having the luxury to be able to be gone, away from home and business, at various times during the year for extended periods of time, is an altogether different type of reward, yet attainable for you if you're not already there. Remember, you're just as close or as far away from whatever target it is that you're shooting for, depending on how you program your thoughts. Likewise, being wealthy or living in paradise is more of a state of mind than any-thing else as long as you no longer have to trade time for money.

Having Peace of Mind and Freedom of Movement

Once your passive income exceeds a certain level on a very consistent basis, with virtually no more financial worries, you begin to experience the greatest feelings of all—total peace of mind and freedom of movement. Though there are dangers in letting your mind go blank, always remembering that "an idle mind is a devil's workshop," you will all of a sudden find time to do things, time that you were unable to find before. You soon will accept your new situ-ation, and you will begin to practice peaceful activity. You will pace yourself better, you will trim your schedule, you will truly get orga-nized, you will plan escapes, you will realize complete wholeness within yourself, and complete peace of mind and freedom of move-ment will be upon you.

What a terrific feeling financial freedom brings. You also become much better at setting boundaries, being better able to say no to people who always ended up wasting your time in the past. You will also feel as though you've regained parts of your sanity that you thought were lost forever, you'll become a master at blocking time so that you have a much better shot at completing certain tasks that you put on hold many years before, and you will find tranquility and patience like never before observed or encountered.

Being able to mentally get away from it all and keep things simple will do wonders to restore your faculties and allow you to achieve the truest forms of peace of mind and freedom of movement.

Leaving a Legacy

Leaving a legacy is something many people consider once they decide to make their mark on the world. And, of course, "the size of their splash" is usually determined by the amount of riches they have accumulated during their lifetime, by the type of scholarship they set up financed through fundraisers, or through their wisdom, discoveries, or creations that perpetually empower others.

Perhaps you too will find a way to leave some form of legacy that affects untold numbers of people for many generations to come. Though I haven't yet made my greatest "splash" on the world, I do plan to continue furthering my message for as long as I'm alive and hopefully for a very long time into the future. At this point I only know that I'm very staunchly opposed to waste and that the mere thought of wastefulness of any kind really gets my attention! Also, it's not only simple waste like that of food and consumer goods that drives me crazy, but massive industrial waste taking place on a large scale all around us, as well as the destruction of our environment and the polluting of our lands, rivers, lakes, and oceans, that really has me worried about the survival of our loved ones, of future generations, and of all mankind.

Hopefully, by the time my life comes to an end, I will have been able to write enough books, make enough films, or deliver enough speeches on the topics of wastefulness, going green, or scavenging recyclable materials to have made some difference in the world. That recognition for my life's passion in itself would be the biggest reward, scavenged or otherwise, I could ever hope to receive, posthumously or otherwise. Perhaps you, too, for whatever it is you firmly stand for, can have a positive impact on the world, at least in some way, by striving to be your best, by inspiring excellence in others, and by making your life about something bigger than yourself.

Key Points

- A passive income stream can provide more freedom to enjoy life. You can retire early or work when you want, as much as you want, when you want to.
- Property appreciation can be slow, but over time these investments are less risky and more steady than other options. Also, much of this appreciation may be tax free.
- Buy a few interesting collectibles that you enjoy. They're nice to have, and one day your heirs may also enjoy them or be able to sell off the collection for a high price.
- With enough passive income, you can take long vacations and have enough time to really appreciate the area.
- You can't take it with you when you die, but you can leave scholarships, books, and videos you've created and other long-lasting things to improve the lives of future generations

I hope you've enjoyed the book. Please be advised that more books and e-books, audio programs, DVD programs, CDs, etc. will soon be available on our website www.scavengercentral.com.